Take delight in the LORD,
And he will give you the desires of your heart.

—PSALM 37:4 (NIV)

SECRETS *From* GRANDMA'S ATTIC

History Lost and Found
The Art of Deception
Testament to a Patriot
Buttoned Up
Pearl of Great Price
Hidden Riches
Movers and Shakers
The Eye of the Cat
Refined by Fire
The Prince and the Popper
Something Shady
Duel Threat
A Royal Tea
The Heart of a Hero
Fractured Beauty
A Shadowy Past
In Its Time
Nothing Gold Can Stay
The Cameo Clue

The Cameo Clue

Shirley Raye Redmond

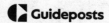

Secrets from Grandma's Attic is a trademark of Guideposts.

Published by Guideposts
100 Reserve Road, Suite E200
Danbury, CT 06810
Guideposts.org

Copyright © 2023 by Guideposts. All rights reserved.

This book, or parts thereof, may not be reproduced, stored in a retrieval system, or transmitted in any form or by any means, electronic, mechanical, photocopying, recording, or otherwise, without the written permission of the publisher.

This is a work of fiction. While the setting of Secrets from Grandma's Attic as presented in this series is fictional, the location of Canton, Missouri, actually exists, and some places and characters may be based on actual places and people whose identities have been used with permission or fictionalized to protect their privacy. Apart from the actual people, events, and locales that figure into the fiction narrative, all other names, characters, businesses, and events are the creation of the author's imagination and any resemblance to actual persons or events is coincidental.

Every attempt has been made to credit the sources of copyrighted material used in this book. If any such acknowledgment has been inadvertently omitted or miscredited, receipt of such information would be appreciated.

Scripture references are from the following sources: *The Holy Bible, King James Version* (KJV). *The Holy Bible, New International Version* (NIV). Copyright © 1973, 1978, 1984, 2011 by Biblica, Inc. Used by permission of Zondervan. All rights reserved worldwide. www.zondervan.com

Cover and interior design by Müllerhaus
Cover illustration by Greg Copeland at Illustration Online LLC.
Typeset by Aptara, Inc.

ISBN 978-1-961125-89-6 (hardcover)
ISBN 978-1-961125-90-2 (epub)

Printed and bound in the United States of America
10 9 8 7 6 5 4 3 2 1

THE Cameo Clue

Chapter One

Tracy Doyle ventured once again into Grandma Pearl's attic late Sunday afternoon—this time in search of potential props for the church's upcoming Christmas pageant—wondering if she would ever get everything done on her holiday to-do list.

"There's a cheap wooden jewelry box stashed away in a footlocker, as I recall," her aunt Ruth said as Tracy and her sister, Amy, made their way up the stairs. "You can spray-paint the box gold and add some glitter or fake gems. One of the wise men can carry it. Of course, my memory isn't what it used to be. I may have already given that old box away. I'm not as young as I used to be, and neither is my mind. What do I know?"

Amy chuckled, whispering to Tracy, "I've heard that before."

Tracy laughed as she trudged up the narrow steps ahead of her sister. Aunt Ruth had stayed behind to help with dishes following the family's Sunday meal after church. Everyone else had gone home. Miles Anderson, Amy's fiancé, had taken Amy's kids, Matt and Jana, and his own two kids, Colton and Natalie, to the ice-skating rink for an afternoon of fresh air and exercise.

"The footlocker is a burgundy one with silver rivets," Aunt Ruth hollered after them. "Shouldn't be too hard to find."

"Oh, sure, easy for her to say," Amy grumbled, following close on Tracy's heels.

At the top of the stairs, Tracy stopped to catch her breath. She tugged the chain of the overhead light. Gesturing toward the crowded attic room, she declared, "One of these days we're going to have everything up here totally organized."

Amy laughed. "So you keep saying. But we are making progress." She indicated the folding tables and neat piles of items that had already been sorted.

"I mean it this time. We've still got to weed out more stuff." Collectibles were one thing. Junk was another. Tracy glanced around the room, hoping to catch sight of a burgundy footlocker. It was chilly in the attic, but not too cold. The December weather had been warmer than usual. Amy's kids had been praying for snow. Truth be told, most of the kids in Canton were probably praying for snow too.

Amy stepped around her, nearly knocking over a stack of old *National Geographics*. "I'm sure Robin would be happy to help you make an inventory."

Tracy considered this. Amy was right. Their cousin Robin Davisson owned an antique shop called Pearls of Wisdom, and she was their go-to when it came to questions about their attic finds. But Tracy needn't think about that today. She wanted to find the footlocker containing Aunt Ruth's old jewelry box and keep an eye out for anything else that might be used in the pageant. Tracy recalled seeing strands of gold garland that could be used for halos for Jana and the other angels. She'd told Amy about it during lunch, and her sister had volunteered to venture into the attic to help search for it.

"Speaking of Robin," Amy went on, "I guess we won't be going over to her place to celebrate Kai's birthday this year. She said he doesn't want a party. How did he get to be fifteen so fast?" Amy shook her head.

"I don't know," Tracy said. "The kids all seem to grow up in such a hurry these days." She glanced at her watch. "Kai should be playing laser tag with his friends about now."

Kai had asked to skip his traditional birthday hot dog supper and family gathering for cake and ice cream. Instead, he'd requested a laser tag party with a couple of friends from school. This was the day that worked out for everyone, so Jeff and Robin's husband, Terry, had piled the boys into the SUV earlier that afternoon and headed to St. Louis.

"Jeff promised to spring for pizza after," Tracy added, "which was a great idea, because we didn't know what to get Kai for his birthday."

"I gave him a gift card. He can buy what he likes. I'm learning that the older they are, the harder it is to buy for them." Amy opened the drawers in a tall chest, peering inside each one. She pulled out a handful of worn and ratty doilies, yellowed with age, and put them back. "Robin said he's just as happy to have cash or a gift card and do his own shopping."

"Matt's probably getting to the age where he feels that way too," Tracy said. She picked up a small silver teapot, badly tarnished. After looking it over and noticing a dent, she put it down again. No wonder Robin hadn't claimed this for the store yet. Too much work involved to make it marketable.

"Matt's still hoping for that pinball machine he discovered at Robin's," Amy said. "I'd love to get it for him for Christmas, but it's too expensive. And with the thought of what the wedding will cost, I don't think I can afford it. Besides, what he really needs—and Jana too—is underwear, socks, and new pajamas."

"What a fun Santa's helper you are," Tracy teased. "Why don't you let me and Jeff give Matt and Jana those things for Christmas? You can give them the fun stuff. Oh, look." She pointed. "There it is."

Tracy shoved up the sleeves of her sweatshirt, made her way to the footlocker, and leaned over, heaving it away from the wall so Amy could open the lid. It made a rusty squeaking sound as she did so. The faint but pungent odor of mothballs wafted out of the trunk. Tracy wrinkled her nose. Such a nasty smell. She and Amy rummaged through the items inside. The wooden box with its domed lid was found easily enough. Amy removed it, along with an ivory-colored woolen bed jacket—worn and nubby with age. Tracy had a hard time imagining Aunt Ruth wearing it. Or had it been Grandma Pearl's?

"Hey, I can cut the sleeves off this and use it as part of a shepherd's costume," Amy said, sounding pleased.

"What about this?" Tracy lifted a brown waffle-weave blanket from the trunk. It was slightly moth eaten, the satin binding frayed. "We could cut it up to make tunics for a couple of the kids."

Amy squealed. "Perfect. I'll take it."

Tracy glanced into the trunk and noticed an old scrapbook. The cardboard cover must have been navy blue at one time but had since faded to a sickly gray color. She lifted it and saw that the front and back covers were held together by thick black cords that looked like oversized shoelaces.

"What's this?" Tracy opened the book and started turning the heavy pages that were covered with old newspaper articles. The glue had dried out in places, leaving the articles loose and sometimes crumbling at the corners. There was a pink cameo brooch pinned to one of the stiff pages—the silver filigree tarnished with age. The profile of a young woman with cascading ringlets appeared to have been carved from ivory—real ivory or fake? Tracy didn't know which. The newspaper clippings had turned yellow. Some had puckered where the paste had dried underneath. The book smelled musty. All the headlines and following articles shared a common theme: *Who Is the Woman in White?*

Each article—most of them from the *Lewis County Times* and a few from the *St. Louis Dispatch*—appeared to be about the death of an unidentified young woman. There was even a police sketch of her included with one article.

"Who is she?" Amy asked, peering over Tracy's shoulder.

"I don't know." Tracy read the caption, printed in bold capital letters. "'Police Seek Help in Identifying Deceased Woman.'"

"Are all the articles about the same thing?" Amy probed.

Tracy nodded. "I think so. I've only scanned the headlines, but they all seem to have something to do with this young woman who died in Canton, and no one knew who she was."

"When did this happen?"

Tracy noted a date in the corner of one of the articles. "December 1944."

"Then it can't be Aunt Ruth's scrapbook," Amy declared. "She wasn't even born yet."

Tracy frowned. "True. So maybe it was Grandma Pearl's."

Amy shrugged. "Or Grandpa Howard's."

Tracy chuckled. "I can't imagine Grandpa Howard sitting in the barracks somewhere with a jar of paste, cutting articles like this out of the newspaper."

With a smile, Amy admitted, "I guess you're right."

"Odd, though, that Grandma Pearl never mentioned this—if it belonged to her. Someone else could have cut out the articles and given the scrapbook to her." Tracy closed the book, determined to look at it more carefully later on. "Are you done rummaging through the trunk?"

Amy nodded.

Tracy hugged the scrapbook to her chest with one hand and closed the lid of the old trunk with the other.

"Grandma and Grandpa didn't talk much about World War II unless we prodded them," Amy pointed out. "And I don't remember Mom and Dad talking about the events of the fifties and sixties much." She shrugged as she gathered up the items she'd found. "Come to think of it, I'm not sure I've talked to Matt and Jana about 9/11 either—it gets mentioned at school, but we don't discuss it. If Grandma Pearl did keep that scrapbook, I suppose she could have eventually forgotten all about the incident surrounding the woman's death. It's not the kind of thing that comes up in daily conversation."

Tracy thought about that. Amy had a point.

They spent another fifteen minutes scrounging for odds and ends that might be useful for the pageant before making their way back downstairs. They found Aunt Ruth sitting on the couch in the living room, perusing Amy's three-ring binder—the one containing all the inspiration she'd gathered so far for her wedding.

"Hey, I thought you were going to sort through those Christmas decorations," Tracy said. She pointed to a box on the coffee table that she had brought down from the attic a week ago. With Christmas only two weeks away, it was time to finish decorating the old house the way Grandma Pearl used to. Aunt Ruth loved to help. Doing so brought back many fond memories for her. After all, she'd grown up in this house.

"I intended to." Aunt Ruth shrugged. "But I couldn't resist Amy's binder. You're so well organized," she said, smiling at her niece.

Amy smiled back. "I try. I really do."

Tracy held up the dusty scrapbook. "Ta-da! Look what we found in that old footlocker, Aunt Ruth."

"What is it, dear?"

Tracy thrust it toward her. "It's a scrapbook about some mysterious young woman who died in Canton in December of 1944. Apparently, nobody knew who she was. Do you know if this belonged to Grandma Pearl? Did she cut out all the articles?"

Aunt Ruth took the scrapbook and opened it. As she touched the old cameo brooch, her eyes widened and she blinked rapidly. Her mouth dropped open, her shoulders began to shake, and to Tracy's dismay, her aunt burst into tears.

Chapter Two

Tracy's heart seemed to drop to her knees. Amy's mouth gaped open. The two of them exchanged concerned glances. What on earth had upset Aunt Ruth? Was it possible that she knew something about the mysterious Woman in White? It seemed unlikely, since the incident had taken place before Aunt Ruth was even born. Amy dumped the old jewelry box and other items onto the coffee table, dashed to the dining room, and grabbed a box of tissues from the sideboard. Tracy put an arm around her aunt's heaving shoulders. Sadie wagged her tail nervously, unsure of what was going on.

"Aunt Ruth, I'm so sorry. I didn't mean to upset you. Come into the kitchen and let me get you a cup of coffee or tea. I have that peppermint brand you like."

Accepting a tissue from the box Amy held out, Aunt Ruth gave a watery sniff and nodded her thanks. She allowed Tracy to lead her to the kitchen. Tracy still had the scrapbook tucked under one arm. When Amy gave her another anxious look, arching her eyebrows, Tracy grimaced. Had she known the scrapbook would cause such a reaction, she wouldn't have shown it to her aunt without finding out first what it was all about.

As Amy pulled out a chair at the kitchen nook and settled Aunt Ruth comfortably, Tracy slipped a tea bag into a mug full of water and popped it into the microwave. No time to heat up the kettle now.

"I'm sorry to be such a blubber baby," their aunt apologized after blowing her nose and wiping her eyes. "I guess I'm feeling sentimental. It's that time of year, you know. Being here in the house surrounded by your grandmother's Christmas decorations and remembering her passing, I suppose I'm overwhelmed by memories and feeling just a little bit blue."

Tracy hugged her. "We understand." She kept her tone low and soothing. Tracy couldn't help feeling a little sentimental herself. It was that time of year. When the microwave dinged, she retrieved the mug and carried it to her aunt. She then pushed the sugar bowl and a teaspoon toward her.

"Did the scrapbook bring back sad memories? Is it yours?" Amy asked, settling into a chair across from Aunt Ruth. Sadie wriggled underneath the table, resting her chin on her front paws. "We found it in the same footlocker where you'd stashed your jewelry box."

Aunt Ruth shook her head. "No, it was your grandmother's. She showed it to me once or twice over the years. Seeing it again… It made me realize how much I miss her." She gave another watery sniff. "Don't mind me. I'm being silly. Really, I'm fine. Just a little embarrassed now, that's all."

Tracy felt a lump in her throat. She missed Grandma Pearl too—especially at Christmastime. She'd died almost two years ago on the day after her one hundredth birthday. Everywhere Tracy looked, she could see something that had once belonged to her beloved grandmother—the old silver Christmas tree in the living room, the nativity sets, the antique letters to Santa mailbox, the brilliant chandelier that Jeff had insisted be restored to its former splendor. Even the divinity recipe written in Grandma Pearl's own hand that was propped on the counter beside the toaster.

"So, Grandma cut out the newspaper articles about the dead woman and pasted them in?" Amy asked. "It seems like such a grim event to keep a scrapbook about."

"Yes, the incident took place in 1944. Mother and Dad weren't even married yet, and the country was embroiled in World War II." Aunt Ruth's voice was low and husky. She cleared her throat. "It bothered Mother for years afterwards that no one ever came forward to identify that poor young woman now buried in the local cemetery. As I recall, the woman arrived by bus, collapsed on the sidewalk, and died shortly afterwards. They said she'd been very ill. You can read all about it in the clippings."

Aunt Ruth pointed to the scrapbook. More tears welled in her eyes as she took another tissue from the box. She gave a ragged sigh and stared out the kitchen window, apparently lost in thought for a moment.

Tracy felt a tug of sympathy and could feel the frown lines creasing her forehead. She and Amy exchanged worried glances again. It was not like Aunt Ruth to demonstrate such emotion—she was a no-nonsense sort of gal. Was it possible that there was more to the scrapbook than just a collection of old newspaper clippings? Was their family related to the deceased woman somewhere along the line?

"Go on, Aunt Ruth," Amy urged. "What else can you tell us?"

Tracy realized then that Amy was as intrigued by the unusual story as she was.

The Cameo Clue

"I had to write a term paper for my social studies class, something with a Missouri theme," Aunt Ruth continued. "Mother suggested I write about the Woman in White. They dubbed her that because she'd been wearing a white coat. Winter white, don't you know? Mother gave me the scrapbook to start my research." She sipped her tea. "But my teacher didn't think the incident had enough historical significance. She preferred that I pick another topic. I decided to write about Lewis and Clark beginning their westward exploration from St. Louis. I gave the scrapbook back to Mother and never saw it again."

Aunt Ruth pulled the scrapbook across the table. She flipped the stiff pages to the one with the police sketch of the unidentified woman and pointed to it. "She was pretty, wasn't she? Like I said, your grandmother seemed disturbed by the fact that no one ever stepped forward to give her a name. No one ever claimed her as a friend or family member. No one ever has, as far as I know."

"It's a shame," Amy declared softly. She leaned forward to get a better look at the sketch.

"I'm surprised there are no photographs of her. Just a sketch in the scrapbook," Tracy observed. "Or maybe Grandma Pearl couldn't find a photo of the woman in the local paper."

With a shrug and a wan smile, Aunt Ruth added, "The county ended up burying the woman because no one ever stepped forward to identify her. I don't remember all the details."

"It's really odd that no one identified her." Tracy tapped the sketch, now yellow with age. "She must have been coming to Canton to see someone. It says she got off the bus here."

"Or Canton was her home, and she was returning here for the holidays," Amy pointed out. "If that's true, someone in town had to know her. She must have had friends, neighbors, family members—perhaps even an employer or a husband. Someone."

Aunt Ruth lifted a shoulder in a shrug.

"That's right," Tracy said. "Even if she had no relatives, surely a boss would report a missing employee who never showed up for work. Someone here should have been able to identify her. And if that someone didn't do so, you've got to wonder why."

That was a nice thing about a small town. It would be hard for someone to fall through the cracks. It could happen, of course, but not as often as it would in a big city where people didn't always know their neighbors. In Canton, if someone didn't bring in their mail or pick up their newspaper from the front lawn, neighbors would notice and do some checking.

Tracy reached over to turn a few more pages. "What about this cameo brooch? Did it belong to the unidentified woman? It's very similar to the one in the sketch."

"I think it's the same one," Aunt Ruth replied, "but I'm not sure."

Tracy gave her a puzzled look. "Then why would Grandma Pearl have it?"

Aunt Ruth shook her head. "I don't know that either, Tracy. Truly. Read the articles. You'll learn everything there is to know—or at least everything there was to know at the time."

"Are you certain that Grandma Pearl didn't know this woman, or know something about her?" Amy probed. "It seems odd that she would have taken the woman's cameo and cut out articles about her death. It's unlike Grandma to take such an interest in a total stranger, don't you think?"

The Cameo Clue

Tracy disagreed and said so. "No, it's just the sort of thing Grandma Pearl would do. She had a heart the size of Texas. She probably felt a great deal of sympathy for the young woman who died so tragically. If this sketch is accurate, the two of them must have been close in age."

"I feel certain Mother didn't know anything about this woman, or she would have said so at the time, and then the young lady wouldn't have been buried without a name on her tombstone," Aunt Ruth pointed out. "Maybe your grandmother discovered something scandalous later down the road and decided to let sleeping dogs lie. I really have no idea."

Amy reached for the scrapbook and flipped through a few pages. "They referred to her as the Woman in White because of her clothes?"

"That's what it says in one of the articles," Tracy said. "Like Aunt Ruth just said, she arrived in Canton wearing a winter-white dress and a matching wool coat."

"I read a novel with that title in college in my British Lit class," Amy said. "*The Woman in White* by Wilkie Collins."

"If you're really interested, read the articles in there," Aunt Ruth repeated, pointing to the scrapbook.

"It says here in one of these articles that someone regularly placed white roses on her grave. I think that's rather romantic, don't you think?" Amy mused. "I wonder who did so and why? And wouldn't someone have discovered who'd brought them?"

"White carnations would have been cheaper," Tracy pointed out, ignoring her sister's many questions. "I wonder if flowers were rationed during the war."

Amy snorted. Her mouth quirked up in a playful grin. "I doubt it."

"Who knows?" Tracy insisted. "Everything else was rationed—sugar, butter, shoes, meat." Jeff would know. She'd ask him. History was his profession. If he didn't know what might have been rationed during World War II, he'd certainly know where to dig up the information.

"If this happened back in 1944, maybe someone has stepped forward to identify the woman since these articles appeared in print," Amy suggested as she turned another page. "After all, it's been what—almost eighty years?"

"I don't know what has gone on since then," Aunt Ruth said. "Until you found this scrapbook, I'd completely forgotten about it. I certainly haven't heard folks talking about it recently." The wrinkles deepened between her eyes.

Tracy contemplated the remark. She hadn't heard about the Woman in White incident either. Why not? Was it possible that someone had refused to step forward to identify the young woman? If so, why would they do such a thoughtless thing?

"You ought to take the scrapbook next door to Columbia and see what she has to say about it," Aunt Ruth suggested. "I wouldn't be surprised if Mother talked to Columbia about it at one time or another. They were always thick as thieves, those two."

Tracy nodded. "Good idea."

Grandma Pearl and Columbia Burke had been great friends for years, despite the difference in their ages. Now a widow in her late seventies, Columbia certainly might know something about the incident, even though it had taken place before she was born.

Shortly afterward, Amy left with the items she'd collected from the attic, offering to give Aunt Ruth a ride home. With hugs and promises to see Tracy soon, Amy and Aunt Ruth left, with Sadie trailing them to the front door. Tracy wanted to see Columbia right away, but first she went to the bathroom to wash her hands and tidy up her hair. The mirror confirmed she'd ventured into the dusty attic. She had a smudge on one cheek and a piece of unidentifiable fluff in her hair. From that old bed jacket possibly? After making herself presentable, Tracy brushed off her shoulders and adjusted her sweatshirt.

She snatched a heavy jacket from the hall closet and walked next door to see Columbia, taking the faded scrapbook with her. She knocked on the door, which sported an attractive evergreen wreath decorated with red ribbons and fake candy canes. Columbia opened the door. She smiled broadly, causing soft wrinkles around her bright hazel eyes.

Before Tracy could say a word, her neighbor glanced down at the scrapbook. "I've often wondered when that might turn up again," she said. "It's Pearl's Woman in White scrapbook, isn't it?"

June 11, 1944

Peoria, Illinois

Dear Aunt Violet,

I know you must be surprised to hear from me, since I haven't written in over a year. So much has happened since then, and none of it too good. I need your help. I really do. I hate to ask for a favor, but I don't know where else to turn. My husband, Tom, has been killed in action—his ship was torpedoed in the Pacific somewhere. The Western Union telegram, sent by the Secretary of War no less, didn't contain any details. It said a letter would follow. But what do I care about the details? Tom is dead. Now I am alone in the world. I'm at my wit's end trying to figure out what to do.

My widow's pension won't be enough to live on, so I don't intend to give up working. Right now, I have a job at the local movie theater working in the ticket booth. I enjoy it. I get to see all the films for free, but the hours are long because we open in the morning at eleven and close at midnight. It's tiring, I'll admit. Besides that, I've developed a bothersome cough. Guess I let myself get run down after receiving the grim news about Tom. My heart is broken. We had such beautiful dreams, such wonderful plans. I still find it hard to believe he's never coming back.

I'm feeling mighty blue, Aunt Vi. Would you mind if I came to Canton to stay with you and Uncle Alfred for a while? And cousin Dorinda too. I used to call her Dory Dearie, remember? She must be quite a big girl by now. What is she—ten or twelve? Or is she thirteen and already a teenager? As you'll recall, I was just a teenager myself when you came to Peoria to see Mom and me.

I've been thinking about all of you a great deal of late. It's an odd feeling not to belong to anyone and not to have anyone belong to me. As you know, you're the last kinfolk I have left since Mom passed away. I could take the train to St. Louis and then come the rest of the way by bus and stay with you and Uncle Alfred for a while. I've never been across the river, but I'm sure Canton is real nice.

Please, Aunt Violet, I don't know what else to do or where to go. I promise I won't be a bother. I can share a room with Dory or sleep on the sofa—whatever you can offer. I'll bring my ration book, of course. I don't eat much these days anyway. I seemed to have lost my appetite even before learning of Tom's death. Maybe Uncle Alfred could help me find a job. Do you think he could? I'm willing to do just about anything if I know how. And even if I don't know, I can learn. I'm quick that way.

My Tom had no folks either. He was raised in an orphanage somewhere in Ohio. I never thought I'd end up a widow at twenty-one. I didn't reckon on Tom dying in the war. What was I thinking? Foolish me! In my daydreams, I imagined Tom coming home looking so handsome in his uniform and sporting all sorts of medals and ribbons on his chest. Heavenly day! I've been such a fool.

Do you still have the wedding photograph I mailed to you last year? Then you know what a handsome guy my Tom was. We got married at the courthouse by a justice of the peace. I believe I mentioned that in the letter. Did you notice I wore Mom's old cameo brooch, the one Grandma Herman passed on to her? That was the traditional "something old." My light gray suit was "something new." My cute little hat was dark blue, and a friend loaned me a lacy handkerchief for "something borrowed." I covered all the bases, Tom said. Ha, ha. I will treasure the memory of that happy day forever.

I had to move out of the little apartment Tom and I shared before he joined up. To be quite honest, I couldn't afford it any longer. I'm living now in a boardinghouse for unmarried women. I like it. Everyone is quite friendly. I share a room with a sweet gal from Linton, Indiana. Her name is Jilly. She works in the Holmes and Edwards factory. They used to make sterling inlaid silverplate spoons and forks and things like that, but not now. It's all war work for the military. Anyway, Jilly's a good sort and puts up with my coughing at all hours. She says she can sleep through anything, and I believe her. Like me, she works long hours and is plumb tuckered out by the end of her shift.

Aunt Vi, I know you to be a kind Christian woman familiar with the Good Book and what it says about widows and orphans. My mother—God rest her soul—was too, as you know, being her sister and all. I guess I'm feeling homesick for family now that I've lost my Tom. It's a miserable feeling.

Don't worry about me cluttering up your place with my things. I don't have much—only a few bits and bobs. Tom and I weren't married all that long, and our little apartment came furnished. I just need someplace to stay until I can catch my breath, so to speak. Tom's death knocked me for a loop, I'll admit it. Also, I'm feeling a little poorly on top of the grieving. This nasty cough takes the sap right out of me.

If you could write back to me real soon in care of Mrs. Batterson's Boardinghouse for Respectable Women, I'd be ever so grateful. The address is up in the corner of the envelope.

Talk it over with Uncle Alfred, okay? And see what he says.

Please write soon.
Your loving niece,
Trula

Chapter Three

"Come on in, Tracy. Get out of the cold." Columbia opened her front door wide. She looked cheery in a pink polar fleece pullover with a white turtleneck underneath. She and her late husband, Charles, had lived next door to Grandma Pearl for decades. Columbia had also written the Cantonbury Tales column for the *Lewis County Times* for more years than Tracy could remember. There wasn't much about Canton that Columbia didn't know. She'd been a good mentor when Tracy had decided to pursue a journalism career.

"So, you have seen this before?" Tracy asked, indicating the warped scrapbook as she followed Columbia to the living room.

"Yes indeed, but it's been a good many years. Where did you find it? No, wait. Don't tell me. Let me guess. Up in your grandmother's attic." Columbia grinned.

Tracy grinned back. "Yep, you guessed it. Now tell me what you know."

A fake fire danced in the fireplace. But the scent of fresh gingersnaps was quite real. Tracy's stomach rumbled. It had been a while since lunch. Besides, rummaging around in Grandma Pearl's attic always seemed to make her hungry. Tracy was delighted when Columbia urged her to come into the kitchen where she offered her hot coffee and warm cookies.

The Cameo Clue

"Or would you prefer eggnog?" Columbia asked. "Not home-made, I should mention. Out of a carton."

"Coffee would be perfect," Tracy assured her. She pulled out a green vinyl chair at the square kitchen table and sat down. She glanced around the kitchen, noticing that most of the countertops were covered with cookies cooling on parchment paper. It was a cheerful room in warm shades of brown and green with a pine cone motif in the curtains, dish towels, and even the coffee mugs and plates.

Columbia placed a steaming cup of coffee in front of Tracy. "You must have dozens of questions. Help yourself to the cookies. As you can see, I have plenty." Columbia gestured to the crowded countertops.

"Christmas baking already?" Tracy asked, smiling. The scent that wafted through the room made her mouth water. With almost two weeks left to go, Tracy hadn't begun to think about baking yet, and she always waited until the last minute to make Grandma Pearl's divinity. "They should make an air freshener that smells as good as your kitchen does right now."

"My ladies Bible study group is having a cookie swap," Columbia informed her. "They all love my cookies best. I use old recipes and make my cookies from scratch. None of that ready-made cookie dough for me. Besides, the grandkids are coming for a few days over Christmas." She beamed. "I want to enjoy them while they're here, so I'm getting a head start on baking and wrapping presents and all that."

Tracy reached for a soft molasses crinkle then tapped the scrapbook with one hand and said, "Okay, tell me what you know about this."

"Let me see now. It was a long, long time ago. I'd just been hired on at the paper. So that would make it about 1969. I was young and eager to make a name for myself." Columbia chuckled softly as she sat down across from Tracy. "Pearl wanted me to write a 25th-anniversary article about the Woman in White. She talked me into interviewing several Canton residents who'd been involved in some way with the incident, like the doctor and the minister who did the burial. My editor gave his approval, and I delved into the story, focusing mainly on the white roses that appeared on the grave site each December. Some of the other newspapers in the region did the same, printing anniversary articles. It was quite a mystery, even after all those years. Still is an unsolved mystery, I guess."

"So even then, after twenty-five years, no one had stepped forward to identify the young woman?" Tracy was flabbergasted.

Columbia leaned back in her chair. "No one stepped forward, but people kept trying to discover who she was. Your grandmother tried. The police tried too. They even published a sketch and had that circulated in the area newspapers as far north as Chicago."

After taking a sip of coffee, Tracy said, "I've seen the sketch in here. I'm curious, though, why they didn't take a photograph."

"I believe there's a morgue photo somewhere. The police required one for their investigation. Don't know if that was ever shared with the public, however." Columbia paused, pursing her lips. "I remember my editor receiving a letter from a couple in Arkansas. Said they'd seen the sketch and thought the girl might be their daughter. They asked if any cash was found in her purse." Columbia snorted. "My editor turned the letter over to the police."

"Then what happened?"

With a shrug, Columbia went on. "Don't know for sure, but we heard through the grapevine that the couple apparently just wanted to claim any belongings that the woman had. Anything of value. As far as I know, the police couldn't or didn't hand anything over to them. They couldn't prove the young woman was their daughter. They had no dental records or anything. They couldn't correctly describe any details of the cameo either."

"Do you think she *was* their daughter?" Tracy asked around a bite of cookie.

Columbia shook her head. "I don't think so. They gave up easily enough."

Tracy opened the scrapbook at random. "My grandmother was really intrigued by the whole thing, wasn't she?"

"Yes, for years she wondered why no one ever claimed the poor girl as their own. Pearl was a young woman at the time the Woman in White arrived in Canton, not yet married to your grandpa. For a while, it consumed her thoughts. She just couldn't accept the fact that someone could slip through the cracks like that. The poor girl was sick too. And then she died suddenly with no one to mourn her."

"She died without telling anyone her name?" Tracy found this hard to believe. "Surely someone asked."

"According to the doctor's report, she never regained consciousness after collapsing."

Tracy sighed. "I wish Grandma Pearl had talked to me about this before she died. There are so many questions I would have liked to ask. I wonder why she never brought it up."

"Life goes on," Columbia said. She traced the rim of her coffee mug with a gnarled finger. "Your grandmother was a busy woman."

She reached for the scrapbook, and the two of them sat in companionable silence for a while as she perused its pages.

Tracy tried another angle. "Do you think somebody knew about the young woman—who she was—and wanted it hushed up? Maybe they didn't want anyone to know why she'd come to Canton in the first place."

Columbia frowned. Without looking up from the pages she was skimming, she said, "I'm not sure where you're going with that line of questioning. Are you suggesting the woman was involved in a scandal? With someone here in Canton?"

"It's a thought." Tracy's imagination could conjure all sorts of scenarios. "What if she was someone's illegitimate daughter? Or what if Grandma thought the woman looked familiar—someone she'd met in Camp Fire Girls years before?"

"We'll never know now, I reckon," Columbia said, glancing up from the scrapbook.

"I wonder if Grandma Pearl wanted me to pursue this mystery?" Tracy took a sip of coffee. "As far as I can recall, she never even mentioned the Woman in White. At least not to me."

"Weren't you a nurse when your kids were little?" Columbia tipped her head to one side. "I'm sure it never crossed Pearl's mind to bring it up while you were raising your children. Life can be a handful." She sighed. "And Pearl may have simply forgotten all about it over time. I'm afraid I can't tell you much more than that. Maybe you should try Tawny Hagstrom. There's not much that's happened in this town that she doesn't know something about, especially if it made the headlines."

"Good idea." Tracy made up her mind to speak with Tawny, who ran the Canton Historical Society. She had often proved helpful

The Cameo Clue

when it came to tracking down things in the archival collection. The topic might make a good story for her column.

Columbia added, "Don't forget to check the newspaper archives next time you go to the office too. You shouldn't have any problem finding plenty of information there. More than you'll be able to use, I'm guessing." Tapping the scrapbook, she said, "Your grandmother cut out a lot of articles, but not all those that appeared in print."

Tracy realized that had to be true. The mysterious woman must have been front page news in Canton for days and then inside news for weeks. She made a mental note to check the newspaper archives as soon as possible. She'd start with papers dating back to December 1944. The war was on. With reports of soldiers missing in action and rationing and the general unease in the country, people already had a lot to worry about. Considering the times, perhaps the identity of one young woman wasn't so important after all.

"Tracy, I don't want to rain on your parade," Columbia said, "but you do realize the incident happened nearly eighty years ago, don't you? It's a cold case."

Cold, indeed. Really cold.

"You're right. And frankly, I don't even know where to start." Tracy heaved another sigh. "I guess I should read these articles all the way through more carefully." She opened the scrapbook to the page where the cameo was pinned. "Maybe I can discover something about this brooch." She detached it carefully so as not to tear the brittle page and passed it to Columbia. "I'm surprised they didn't bury the woman with this. She's wearing it in the sketch."

Peering at the brooch closely, Columbia said, "They held on to it, hoping it would be helpful in identifying the woman later.

SECRETS FROM GRANDMA'S ATTIC

They were thinking it could be a family heirloom or something special."

"But how did Grandma come to have it?" Tracy helped herself to another cookie.

Columbia shrugged. "Good question. If Pearl told me, I've forgotten." After taking a sip of coffee, she added, "Although, now that I think about it, when you went to work for the *Lewis County Times*, Pearl mentioned the scrapbook to me again. She considered giving it to you and asking if you would be willing to pursue the story."

Surprised, Tracy sat up straighter. "She did? But she never mentioned it to me. Not once. And she certainly never showed me this scrapbook. I wonder why she changed her mind."

With a shake of her head, Columbia said, "I just don't know. Your grandmother was on the committee that erected the headstone, and she had a definite opinion about the words that should be put on that young woman's gravestone. Originally, they were going to put something like 'the Lost Woman' or 'the Unknown Woman.' Pearl insisted that no one was ever truly lost or unknown—that God knew exactly who she was. 'His eye is on the sparrow,' and so on and so forth."

"There's a photo of the tombstone with one of the articles." Tracy brushed a crumb from the front of her sweatshirt.

Columbia nodded. "She's buried right here in Canton," she said, and mentioned one of the cemeteries on the west side of town.

Tracy decided to visit the grave as soon as possible. Not that she expected to find a clue hidden in the words on the stone, but she felt it would be a good place to launch her investigation. "Well, I guess I'd better get going on this," she said, standing up to take her leave.

26

The Cameo Clue

"I should put it off until the Christmas festivities are over and my schedule clears, but I'm intrigued enough to want to tackle Grandma Pearl's mystery right now."

"Isn't your sister getting married next month?" Columbia asked. "You might have to wait until after the wedding before you plunge into this investigation." Piling cookies onto a festive green-and-red paper plate, Columbia added, "Tracy, you might even want to reconsider pursuing this at all. Read the articles first, then think about it carefully before you go chasing a lead."

"Why?" Tracy picked up the scrapbook and gave Columbia a puzzled frown.

"Maybe Pearl dropped the whole matter because she'd come to realize that someone might get hurt." Columbia handed her the plate of cookies wrapped with foil. "Maybe she uncovered a scandal—or thought she did. Just be careful. Some folks have skeletons in their closets. They might want to keep them in there to preserve their reputations or to protect someone else's. They may even want to keep someone from heartbreak."

With Columbia's words at the back of her mind, Tracy hurried home through the cold, carrying the paper plate loaded with molasses crinkles. Despite her friend's grim warning, Tracy felt invigorated. There was something about grabbing hold of a new mystery that always made her feel charged up. And she needed a bit of charging up because Christmas had its sad moments, despite the many joyful festivities. She missed her parents sorely at this time of the year. Now she missed Grandma Pearl too. That sense of loss never seemed to go away, not completely. It lingered among the scent of holiday cookies and the precious sound of her grandchildren's laughter.

SECRETS FROM GRANDMA'S ATTIC

Still, Tracy resolved to investigate the mystery of the Woman in White. For all she knew, the young woman may have finally been identified years ago. Grandma Pearl may not have been aware of that fact. On the other hand, she may have learned all about it. Was that possible? Perhaps that was why Grandma never passed the scrapbook on to her.

Tracy was determined to find out.

Chapter Four

When Jeff returned home that evening, full of pizza and an animated account of the laser tag war, Tracy listened patiently before finally presenting him with the scrapbook. As they sat together on the couch, munching Columbia's molasses crinkles, Jeff skimmed the stiff and brittle pages. His eyes were wide with interest as she explained about the venture into the attic with Amy and their subsequent discovery.

"When I showed the scrapbook to Aunt Ruth, she started crying."

Jeff arched an eyebrow. "She cried? That's not like Aunt Ruth."

"Her reaction was certainly out of the ordinary. At first I thought it was because of the subject matter. But she said she was feeling mushy because she's missing Grandma Pearl. The old scrapbook made her realize how much. It's that time of year." Tracy felt a pang of loss. She missed Grandma Pearl too.

"I vaguely remember hearing something a long time ago about the Woman in White," Jeff said, reaching for another cookie. "I wonder what your grandmother's connection was to her."

"That's what I'm going to have to find out." Tracy leaned over to see what page he was looking at. "What do you know about her? The unidentified woman, I mean?"

Jeff considered for a moment. "Nothing much. Only that a young woman came to Canton on the bus and died shortly thereafter. Apparently, she was quite ill. No one knew who she was or where she'd come from. No identification in her purse or on her person."

"But she must have been coming to see someone in Canton," Tracy insisted. "Otherwise, why get off the bus here?"

Again, Jeff became pensive. "Don't know," he finally said. "She's buried in one of our cemeteries. I remember that. There's a headstone. I'm not sure who paid for it. I remember seeing a picture of it in the newspaper."

"Yes, it's in there." She pointed to the scrapbook. "That's just one of the questions I have. Another article said the casket was paid for by a church committee, but I'd like to know who served on that committee." Tracy wiped crumbs from the front of her sweatshirt. "In fact, I have a lot of questions."

Jeff smiled at her. "I can almost hear those journalist's wheels turning in your mind."

"I'll just bet you can." Tracy smiled back at him. She appreciated that he was so encouraging of her writing and her research. Come to think of it, she spent more time tracking down interesting material and solving mysteries than she spent writing about them. "I'm going to check this out sooner or later. I need to know why Grandma Pearl kept the scrapbook. What was her interest in the young woman?"

"Did your aunt Ruth know?"

Tracy shook her head.

"What about this cameo?" Jeff touched the old brooch. "It looks like the one the woman is wearing in the police sketch. If it is, why would your grandmother have it?"

The Cameo Clue

"I don't know that either. Neither did Aunt Ruth or Columbia. I suppose I could visit some of the local jewelers and ask about it. Maybe it was purchased here. Maybe someone in Canton purchased the brooch as a gift and there's an invoice somewhere."

Jeff gave a dry chuckle. "You're an optimist. It might be a family heirloom. It's old. Perhaps a lot older than the girl who wore it."

Tracy accepted this in silence. She watched as Jeff turned the pages backward to return to the article with the police sketch of the young woman. The article had come unglued in one corner. He smoothed the clipping as he read it. Tracy studied the sketch over his shoulder. It was a lifelike portrait, well drawn. If it was at all accurate, there was no reason someone couldn't have easily identified the woman.

"A young woman," Jeff observed. "Such a shame to die so young and unmourned by friends and family. It doesn't make sense that no one came forward to identify her."

Tracy nodded. "I agree. But when I mentioned that to Columbia, she hinted there might be a skeleton in someone's closet. She even cautioned me about pursuing this."

"Really?" Jeff stared at her. "What did she mean by that?"

"Don't know exactly."

Tracy decided she might have to have another talk with her neighbor sometime. A sudden chill caused her to shiver. The temperature in the house hadn't plunged. No, it was a sudden and dismaying thought that made her feel cold all over. What if someone had been glad that the young woman was dead? Maybe she'd been blackmailing a Canton resident and they'd kept silent, relieved that she would no longer be a problem. Tracy ventured to say as much to Jeff.

He eyed her suspiciously then burst out laughing. Sadie, lying at his feet, raised her head.

Frowning, Tracy demanded, "What's so funny?"

"You are, sweet pea. What an imagination you have!" Jeff shook his head and continued to turn the pages of the scrapbook. "Blackmail, scandal. All the stuff of a good mystery though."

"Okay, on second thought, it does seem extreme," Tracy admitted. "It's a wild theory. And here's another. Maybe she was a Nazi spy. A German American with ties to the old country. She'd come to meet another spy, who decided he'd better keep mum when the Woman in White collapsed and died."

"I'm not buying it," Jeff mumbled around another bite of cookie. As he continued to peruse one page after another, Tracy chewed her bottom lip. Her thoughts ran amok. There had to be a reason Grandma Pearl had bothered to save all these newspaper articles. Maybe she did suspect a scandal at the time. Hadn't Aunt Ruth cautioned to let sleeping dogs lie and Columbia talked about skeletons in the closet?

"Scandal or not, I think I'll do a little digging," Tracy said, snuggling closer.

Jeff patted her thigh. "Don't be disappointed if you don't come up with anything," he said. "This took place a long, long time ago. The trail has gone cold."

It was true. Columbia had said the same thing. But something about the tragedy had intrigued Grandma Pearl. Perhaps it had troubled her too. Why else would she have mentioned to Columbia that she might have Tracy pursue the story, picking up where she'd left off?

After finishing the cookies—every last crumb—and handing the scrapbook back to Tracy, Jeff retired to their bedroom to watch a special on the History Channel. Tracy tidied up the kitchen and then joined him, bringing the scrapbook with her. She intended to read each article, to study the claims of those interviewed, and learn more about the funeral gathering in the cemetery. She noted right away that not all the articles were from the local paper, which meant Grandma Pearl had gone out of her way to collect some that appeared in other newspapers in the region.

Why had she shown such an interest? It took time to neatly cut out each article and then paste them in the book. And how on earth could anyone go unclaimed in Canton? This was a small town, even back then. A person wouldn't purposefully come here without knowing someone. Even if the woman had had no relatives here, perhaps coming to enroll for the spring semester at the college, surely someone on campus could have helped by suggesting a name. And wouldn't a landlady report the woman missing if she didn't show up as scheduled?

Not only that, the young woman had been sick when she arrived. Seriously sick. Surely someone in the great state of Missouri had provided her with medical attention at one time or another. Why hadn't a doctor or nurse stepped forward to say so? As Columbia suggested, Tracy could begin her research in the newspaper archives. She'd have to check with Tawny at the historical society too. She knew one thing for sure. She wasn't giving up until she had some answers.

SECRETS FROM GRANDMA'S ATTIC

The next morning, after seeing Jeff off to work, Tracy finished a hasty breakfast of Greek yogurt with honey and shaved almonds and then called Annette. The no-nonsense redhead was Tracy's most supportive champion at the paper.

"I'll be in later this morning," Tracy told her. "But first I want to stop by to speak with Tawny Hagstrom."

"Pursuing a story?" Annette probed.

"Maybe. I have some questions about the Woman in White. Have you heard about her? She was buried—anonymously—in one of our local cemeteries in 1944."

Annette gave a slow whistle. "I remember hearing something about it. Our paper has run the occasional anniversary article about those white roses that kept appearing on her grave. But that was all before my time."

"Wait till you see my grandmother's scrapbook," Tracy told her. "You'll understand my interest."

"Okay, see you when you get here. I should warn you. Eric is still angry about something. He's stomping around the office with his knickers in a twist."

"Still? The boss man sure has been crabby lately." Tracy realized that some people were not fond of the hustle and bustle of Christmas, but their editor was proving to be a real Scrooge. He even complained about the goodies people brought to the office to share with the rest of the staff. Who complained about goodies?

"I'll watch my step," Tracy promised.

After snatching up her leather tote bag with her laptop and other work essentials, Tracy slipped on a heavy corduroy jacket, gave Sadie a pat on the head, and then made her way to the Canton

34

The Cameo Clue

Historical Society. It was located in a grand old Victorian home—once the Methodist church parsonage—complete with classic gingerbread trim and a lovely wraparound porch. An evergreen wreath tied with a glittery red bow and laced with tiny Christmas lights graced the front door.

Tracy entered and was immediately greeted by the head curator, who was examining what appeared to be an enormous atlas with one of the part-time docents. "Good morning, Tracy."

"And good morning to you, Tawny," she replied.

"You have that inquisitive gleam in your eye again." Tawny gave her a playful smile and removed her designer glasses. With her bleached-blond hair and trendy royal-blue pantsuit, Tawny looked younger than her sixty-some years. "How can I help you today?"

Tawny had been employed by the historical society for years. Tracy was eager to pick her brain about the Woman in White incident. Before he'd left for the college campus, Jeff had laughingly declared that Tracy was a lot like Sadie with a new bone—she wouldn't be satisfied until she'd given it a good long chew.

"So tell me, Tawny, what do you know about the mysterious Woman in White who arrived in Canton by bus in 1944 and died before anyone got to know her?"

Tawny arched her eyebrows and replaced her glasses on her nose. She folded her arms across her chest. "Now this is curious. Very curious. You're the second person who's come in here asking me that same question. It's been decades since anyone has even brought up the subject, and now two of you in the past week."

Chapter Five

awny cast Tracy a sidelong glance. "Follow me."

She led the way to her small office, calling over her shoulder as she went, "Carry on, Margaret," to the woman still holding the open atlas. The office was lined with shelves. These were stacked with archival boxes and heavy binders containing periodicals and other historical documents. Tracy had been in here before and was familiar with the setting. Tawny left the door partially open and indicated to Tracy to take a seat.

After crossing her legs and leaning back in her swivel chair, Tawny said, "Are you working on a story?"

Tracy held up the scrapbook. "My interest is personal at this point, not professional." While Tawny opened the scrapbook, Tracy glanced at the various items littering her desk. She felt her jaw drop when she noticed a sheet of personalized notepaper with *Eric Watson* printed across the top in bold letters. She clamped her mouth shut again and tried reading his familiar scrawl upside down from where she was seated. It wasn't easy, but she finally made out the words *Canton stage line Kirksville, Culver Stockton,* and *Woman in White.*

Recalling the editor's grumpy behavior of the last several days, Tracy couldn't help but wonder if his mood was connected to his interest in these topics.

Maybe.

But how exactly?

What was Eric up to? His visit to the historical society inquiring about the unidentified woman was certainly a puzzling coincidence. Tracy supposed he could be planning to write a piece commemorating the eightieth anniversary of the incident, but he hadn't mentioned it at the last staff meeting. Besides, that was the sort of story he usually passed off to Tracy or maybe Ed, who covered the Lifestyle section of the paper. What was his interest in the woman if he wasn't, in fact, writing an article about her?

Sometimes digging into the past uncovered secrets—and not all of them pleasant, as she and Amy had learned from experience. Such discoveries could be disturbing. Both Columbia and Aunt Ruth had dropped hints about possible scandals. Was that what Eric was looking into?

"I shouldn't mention the other person by name, but it's quite a coincidence if you ask me," Tawny drawled, lifting an eyebrow and shifting the scrapbook on her lap.

"Indeed it is," Tracy readily agreed. She removed her coat and hung it on the back of the chair. "But as I said, my interest is personal. I'm guessing the other person's inquiry was a professional one." She hoped Tawny would give her a hint.

"I couldn't say," Tawny replied. "We don't have much on the subject, because it wasn't something of actual historical significance. I'm sure your newspaper archive has much more to offer."

Tracy pursed her lips. Curiouser and curiouser, as Alice would say. She wondered what Eric was up to. It certainly was none of her business what he decided to explore.

SECRETS FROM GRANDMA'S ATTIC

Still, his choice of subject right at this time was intriguing.

"So where did you get this?" Tawny asked, holding up the scrapbook.

Tracy explained briefly about her grandmother's fascination with what had happened all those years ago. Even as she uttered the words, she wondered if she should write something on the subject. If Eric found the topic so enthralling, she might score some brownie points by suggesting a story for the next issue. Surely she had enough information in the scrapbook alone to cobble together a quick anniversary piece. If she interviewed a few locals, including Aunt Ruth and Columbia, she might come up with enough reminiscences for an interesting column for Cantonbury Tales. She made a mental note to share her idea with Eric when she got to the office.

"This certainly looks intriguing," Tawny said. Her eyes lit up with pleasure as she perused the pages. "This is a real gem. I'd love to have it for the archives if you don't want it. I wonder why your grandmother was so fascinated." She paused for a moment. "She would have been a young adult at the time, right? Did she know the Woman in White? Were they acquainted somehow?"

Tracy shook her head. "My aunt Ruth says no. Apparently, Grandma Pearl was bothered by the fact that no one came forward to identify the young woman."

Tawny nodded. "Ah, yes. That would be troublesome. Someone should have recognized her."

"There's a police sketch of her in there," Tracy said. "It's my understanding that copies were circulated to newspapers in the state, hoping someone could provide a name—anything."

"Yes, they pursued an investigation of sorts for several months, maybe even a year or more, but finally gave up." Tawny straightened an article that had come unglued then carefully turned the page. "If someone knew who the woman was, they weren't saying."

"I wonder why." Tracy sat back and crossed her legs.

Tawny shrugged. "There have been numerous theories. None of them led to anything though."

Tracy reached for the scrapbook. She flipped to the page with the sketch of the unidentified woman. "What about personal effects? Surely she didn't arrive in Canton empty-handed. Do you have any of those?"

"No, we don't." Tawny gave her a puzzled frown. "Now that you've mentioned it, she must have come to town with something other than the clothes on her back. A suitcase, a handbag, something."

Tracy turned a page or two until she found the one where Grandma Pearl had pinned the cameo brooch. She held up the scrapbook so Tawny could see it. "Look at this. It appears to be the same one the woman is wearing in the sketch. But I can't figure out how my grandmother got hold of it."

"That is odd," Tawny agreed. "You're sure your grandmother didn't know the woman?"

Shaking her head, Tracy said, "Not according to Aunt Ruth. If Grandma Pearl had known her, she wouldn't have let the poor girl be buried without a name on her tombstone."

"Don't you think it's rather unusual for your grandmother to take such an interest in a stranger's death? If I didn't know better, I'd be kind of creeped out." Tawny gave Tracy an apologetic smile. "Pearl put a lot of work into this." She closed the cover of the scrapbook.

"Grandma Pearl was like that," Tracy replied, feeling defensive on her grandmother's behalf. "Like I said, Grandma Pearl was concerned when no one came forward to identify the woman. Columbia Burke told me that my grandmother even toyed with the idea of having me pursue the story after I joined the newspaper staff years ago. But somewhere along the line, Grandma Pearl forgot to tell me."

"Do you think she suspected a scandal of some sort?" Tawny asked, raising an eyebrow.

"Could be."

Just then Tracy heard a familiar voice. A man's voice. Eric Watson was speaking with the docent in the other room. Had he returned to pick up whatever sources Tawny had promised to provide for his research? Tracy lunged to her feet. She scooped up the scrapbook and snatched her coat off the back of the chair. The last thing she wanted was for Eric to see her here, especially if he was in his growling, grumpy mood.

"Is there another door I can sneak out of? A window I can crawl through?" she hissed. "It's Eric. I don't want to see him."

Tracy couldn't explain it, not even to herself, but she didn't think it would bode well for her to run into her boss right now. Not here. She didn't want to have to explain why she was researching the Woman in White incident, just as he had apparently been doing.

Tawny pointed to a door behind her desk that Tracy had supposed was a closet. Tawny opened the door, and Tracy saw that it led to another, smaller, office. "Used to be what's called a sitting room," Tawny said. "And look." She pointed. On the other side of the sitting room was another door with an exit sign over the top. "That will

The Cameo Clue

take you outside to the parking lot where employees and volunteers usually park."

"Thanks, and mum's the word," Tracy said breathlessly.

Tawny gave her a mock salute. "I don't know what you're up to, but I'll disavow any knowledge of your actions."

June 20, 1944
Peoria, Illinois

Trula plopped down in one of the vinyl chairs in Mrs. Batterson's kitchen. At two o'clock in the afternoon, it was almost unbearably warm. The weather had been hot for weeks now—unseasonably so. She dreaded to think what July would be like, not to mention the dog days of August. She rummaged in her apron pocket for her handkerchief, which was already limp from the humidity. Trula used it to pat her flushed cheeks and the beads of sweat on her forehead. Heavens to Betsy, it was hot!

Sighing, she realized just how much she missed her job at the movie theater. But the doctor had insisted she needed rest. Bed rest, specifically. He was concerned about her weight loss and the nasty cough too. He ordered her to take a week off from work. Easy for him to say! Who would pay her rent next month if she didn't bring in some cash? Trula hesitated asking Uncle Alfred and Aunt Violet for money. They hadn't even answered her letter.

Well, that wasn't completely true. Aunt Vi had sent a card of condolence. *So very sorry to hear about Tom's death. It's such a shame,* she'd written. But she'd not included one word about agreeing to let Trula come stay for a while. Not even a hint that a future invitation might be coming. Thanks a heap, Aunt Vi!

Trula hadn't wanted to see the doctor in the first place. It would be just another expense she'd have to bear. But Jilly and Mrs. Batterson both insisted when they saw her coughing up phlegm with a bit of blood. Mrs. B had phoned the doctor herself, suggesting that her young boarder might have pneumonia. *Walking pneumonia,* she called it. The doctor had promised to come around that evening, and he did.

He was a tall man with a head full of bristly red hair and the strangest brown eyes—flat and dark like dirty pennies. He'd given Trula an iron shot and advised her to get bed rest. No, he'd demanded she get bed rest. Real bossy he was about it too. The doctor seemed to think she'd let herself get run down, that grief and fatigue were taking their toll. Said if Trula wasn't better in a week's time, he would order an X-ray. She supposed it would be expensive. How was she to pay for it?

Unable to imagine lying around doing nothing, Trula had asked him, "Can't I help roll bandages or something for the Red Cross?"

"No!" the doctor had snapped. "Bed rest!" He'd then ordered Mrs. B to fatten her up. "She's skinny as a rail," he'd declared with a disapproving glare.

Trula hadn't always been so thin. She'd once been attractively curvy and had known just how to show those curves off to advantage. No doubt about it. She'd always been a welcome addition to the USO dances. That was where she'd met Tom. She'd been wearing that pleated skirt and a polka-dot blouse and red high heels. Very stylish.

Again, Trula sighed. Her clothes were too loose now. Her lips had lost their natural redness, and her face appeared thin and pale. Looking at herself in the mirror was hardly a pleasure anymore. Guess she was more run down than she'd realized. She appeared ghoulish when she tried brightening up her features with lipstick or a touch of rouge. Tom wouldn't know her now, would he? Trula's breath hitched a little, thinking of him, of her painful loss.

Trula rose slowly from the kitchen chair and opened the Frigidaire. She poured herself a glass of lemonade and gulped it down. She could feel the drops dribbling from her chin to the front of her yellow seersucker dress. The wet spots felt cool against her skin. She should be drinking buttermilk. Dr. Henderson insisted she have three glasses a day to help fatten her up. The very thought made her want to gag. Three whole glasses!

Since Mrs. B wasn't here now to enforce the doctor's orders, Trula ignored them. It was bad enough that she had to eat rice pudding twice a day—with raisins. She loathed raisins. Last night at supper, she'd picked them out with her spoon and dropped them into her paper napkin when no one was looking. Raisins reminded her of dead flies. She shuddered. Such a waste of good grapes, in her humble opinion.

No one had noticed her hiding them. At least she didn't think so. Mrs. B and the other women were too enthralled by Sonya Heineman's tale of woe about her nephew's ringworm of the scalp. Trula had never heard of such a thing. However, she soon learned more about it than she ever cared to know. It was caused by a fungus, and it seemed to be inflicting children across the country like an epidemic.

All the women around Mrs. B's dining room table had various theories about the problem. Some felt that parenting had become lax because mothers had gone to work in the factories and other places in support of the war effort. Some blamed the rationing of soap and wholesome food. Rationing can lead to bad hygiene, they insisted.

One of the women surmised it was because of all the bombs and the gunfire, the way warfare munitions poisoned the air. Jilly had laughed out loud at that. She pointed out that no bombs had been dropped in or near Peoria, Illinois,

The Cameo Clue

and that what was happening in Europe and in the Pacific wouldn't have any effect on a fungus here in the States. Later that night, Trula and Jilly had whispered and giggled upstairs in their shared room, amused by the thought of bombs causing a fungus. Jilly said she hoped Hitler and his troops would catch something nasty and call off the war.

Now restless and weary, Trula lowered herself back into the chair. Before she could get settled, she had another one of her coughing spells. She thrust her handkerchief to her mouth, hoping this time there would be no blood in the phlegm. Her hope was in vain. It was there. Blood. Cherry red. She'd need to fetch a clean handkerchief when she could muster the strength to drag herself upstairs.

Trula had watched Mrs. B and a neighbor stoning cherries most of the morning. They canned them too. Hot, sticky work. But it was done now, and the jars glistened like large crimson jewels on the counter. Mrs. B had baked two pies for supper. Trula promised herself to eat an entire slice, even if she didn't feel like it. There would be plenty of pies and cherry cobblers down the road from the looks of things.

Trula hauled herself wearily to the parlor, where a fan circulated the hot air around the room. She lowered herself into an armchair and leaned back against the antimacassar, hoping there was no fungus lingering there.

She shuddered with distaste just thinking about a scalp infection. Trula could see why Jilly would be so concerned about it all. Jilly had gorgeous brown hair. Perfect teeth too. In fact, Trula thought her roommate looked a lot like Deanna Durbin. Jilly was pretty enough to be in a Camay soap ad like the ones in the women's magazines. Jilly had blushed and giggled when Trula told her so. But Trula suspected Jilly was pleased all the same by the compliment.

Oh, how bored she was. And tired. Mrs. B had gone to a friend's house to play canasta. Everyone else was at work. Trula should be upstairs in bed, but it was hotter up there than downstairs. She couldn't bear it. She didn't know what was worse, the heat or the boredom. Trula was never bored at the movie theater. Even when she wasn't selling tickets, there was popcorn to make and the candy counter to keep stocked and whatever other tasks the manager assigned to her.

Trula closed her eyes. It was just too hot to think straight. Mrs. B had brought a paperback book home from the drugstore yesterday. The Case of the Black-Eyed Blonde, *a Perry Mason novel by Erle Stanley Gardner. Trula had noticed it on the end table next to her chair. Mrs. B liked Perry Mason novels, and this one was newly released. Mrs. B insisted entertainment was important with a war on. Movies and books and games were good for morale, she told the girls. Helps keep the spirits up. Trula loved a good mystery story now and then too. But she was too tired to concentrate on reading one, too weary to even open a book.*

Her mind strayed back to her worries about Aunt Violet. Why hadn't her aunt and uncle invited her to come stay? Perhaps she should have given them Mrs. Batterson's phone number, even though she doubted they'd call her long distance. Too costly. That sort of thing was just for emergencies or maybe special occasions. But why hadn't they sent a letter with something more than their condolences?

If the doctor was going to order more bed rest, Trula would just as soon do it at Aunt Vi's home as here. To be fair, Mrs. B had been very kind and sympathetic. She was downright motherly. Still, there would be rent to pay next month. Trula didn't know how much longer she'd be able to afford even sharing a room with Jilly. If she could stay with Aunt Violet, she could do so for free. She supposed so anyway. She hoped so.

Most folks felt sorry for war widows. If Aunt Violet and Uncle Alfred were like most people, they would feel sorry for her too and want to help. Even if they weren't happy about it, they'd feel obligated to do something. Wouldn't they? And Dory? It had been a long time since she'd seen her young cousin. Her only cousin. Dory had been in grammar school at the time and tickled pink to meet Trula, to have a "big girl cousin." That was what Dory had called her.

Dory had followed her around like a young puppy, chattering about this and that, just talking up a storm. That had been several years ago, when her aunt and uncle had come to Peoria to visit. Trula's mother had still been alive then. Dory had brought a shoebox full of paper dolls. Trula still remembered those. Sometimes, especially of late, she wished she was still a girl young enough to play with paper dolls instead of a widow down on her luck.

No!

Stop it!

If Tom were here, he'd tell her, "Don't give way to self-pity, sugar bun."

She had to stop feeling sorry for herself. Now, right this minute. She needed to act cheerful even when she didn't feel that way. Jilly said it was good self-discipline and that if Trula went around bemoaning her circumstances, people would soon grow tired of her griping and not feel sorry for her one little bit.

And if they didn't feel sorry for her, they weren't likely to help her out.

That thought brought Aunt Violet to mind again. Maybe Trula hadn't made her circumstances quite clear enough— that she was sick, her future grim. She needed to write again, be more up front about things.

Trula heaved herself up from the armchair and made her way to the desk in the corner of the parlor. Mrs. B allowed the women the use of the plain stationery she kept there. She even had postage stamps, but each woman was honor bound *to leave three cents on the desk to cover the cost when they took one.*

Trula pulled out the rickety wooden chair and sat down. Wearily, she picked up the blue Parker fountain pen, took a piece of plain white paper from the stationery box, and began writing.

Dear Aunt Violet and Uncle Alfred,

Chapter Six

*T*racy drove to the newspaper office, her heart still racing. She shook her head, feeling slightly ashamed of herself. Good grief! Why had she skipped out like that? She hadn't been doing anything illegal or immoral. Still, she didn't want to run into Eric after the way he'd been grumping around the office lately. If he snapped her head off in front of Tawny—as she feared he might—it would be embarrassing for all concerned. But where were her manners? She hadn't even thanked Tawny for her help. She felt bad that she'd scurried away, leaving the poor woman wondering what was going on.

After angling her way into a parking space, Tracy took the time to remove the cameo from the scrapbook. The pressure of the brooch had caused the brittle page to crack and tear. Tracy slipped it into the secure side pocket inside her purse and then darted into the office of the *Lewis County Times*. She breathed a little easier knowing Eric wasn't present. Passing Jake's desk, she gave the young sportswriter a nod. He was on the phone but took a second to give her a half smile and a nod in return.

"Cranberry-orange muffins in the break room," Bethany Hill chirped as Tracy walked by the young woman's desk. The former intern, now a full-time member of the staff, sported a sprig of holly in her curly brown hair.

The Cameo Clue

Tracy gave her a thumbs-up. "Yum." That was one of the best things about December. Everybody baked and shared what they'd whipped up in their kitchens at home. A Christmas tree with blue and white lights graced one corner of the room—a sparkling reminder of the holiday. Someone had even dressed up the water cooler with a bright red bow.

She intended to stop by Annette's desk to let her know she'd returned from the historical society. Tracy wanted to show her the scrapbook too. Annette had hired her years ago as an assistant, and Tracy considered her more than just a colleague. Annette was a good friend. A quick glance across the room revealed that Annette, who ran the news desk, was also busy talking on the phone. Tracy would have to share the scrapbook with her later.

After placing the scrapbook on the corner of her desk, Tracy removed her winter jacket and plunked down in her chair. She quickly went to work, becoming so absorbed in her various tasks that she wasn't mindful of time passing until her stomach growled. She looked at the clock on the far wall. Almost noon. The only snack in her desk drawer was a half-eaten bag of cheese crackers. Tracy wrinkled her nose. Probably stale and hardly appetizing.

Recalling the mention of cranberry muffins, Tracy decided to take advantage of the treat when Annette approached her. She wore a chunky black turtleneck sweater that set off her red hair to advantage. She carried a puffy blue ski jacket draped over one arm.

"I'm going out for lunch. Want to come with me?"

Tracy didn't have to be asked twice. "Yes, I'm starving."

"Come along then. I've got a craving for hot and sour soup." Annette smiled.

"Sounds good to me." Tracy bounced up so enthusiastically that she accidentally knocked over her pencil mug. Pens, pencils, and markers spilled out over the desk.

"Whoa, Nellie! There's no rush. Take it easy. The food will be waiting when we get there," Annette teased.

"I don't know what's wrong with me today," Tracy said, slipping into her jacket and slinging her purse over her shoulder. "I'm as skittish as a colt." But of course she knew what was wrong. The near encounter with Eric at the historical society had left her on edge. It was ridiculous to feel this way. She needed to get a grip.

In no time at all Tracy and Annette sat across from each other in a booth with creaking, red vinyl bench seats, enjoying the all-you-can-eat Chinese lunch buffet. Annette savored her soup and a heaping plate of rice topped with sweet and sour pork. Tracy dug into a generous serving of shrimp lo mein.

"I don't know why it is, but I'm always hungrier in the winter than in the summer," Annette observed.

"Me too," Tracy agreed. "Maybe it's because we burn more calories putting on coats, gloves, and scarves and then taking them off again."

Annette chuckled. "Sure, that must be it." They both enjoyed several bites before Annette began to probe. "So, what was so important that you had to visit the historical society first thing this morning? You missed Eric's top-of-the-morning tirade. Then he took off but didn't tell any of us where he was going. He's sure turned into a real Scrooge."

Tracy didn't speak at first, her mouth full of savory noodles. She swallowed and took a sip of water before saying, "I'm glad I missed his little...er...pep talk."

The Cameo Clue

Snorting, Annette repeated the words "pep talk" with a roll of her eyes. "He's been in such a bad mood lately. I don't know what's up with him."

Tracy shoveled another bite of noodles into her mouth. After swallowing, she asked, "Do you think the paper is in trouble financially? Maybe that's why he's on edge."

Annette nailed her with a sharp look. "I've not heard anything along those lines. Have you?"

Shaking her head, Tracy said, "No, but I do know where Eric went after he gave the staff his little pep talk."

Annette arched an inquiring eyebrow.

"Believe it or not, Eric arrived at the historical society shortly after I did, while I was speaking with Tawny. We were in her office discussing my grandmother's scrapbook when I heard his voice. I didn't want to run into him there, so I skedaddled out a back door."

"Can't say that I blame you."

Tracy sighed. "I'm sure Tawny thinks I'm crazy. I never even thanked her for her help, but at least she seemed mildly amused. Fact of the matter is, I didn't want to see Eric's glaring face so early in the day. I didn't want to explain why I was there either—not that it's a secret or anything. I wish I knew what's bothering him. He's as prickly as a porcupine."

"Frankly, I don't feel comfortable asking," Annette confessed. After dipping her egg roll into a puddle of sweet and sour sauce, she added quietly, "Rumor has it he's been working on a book. Maybe he's bogged down in his research or maybe he's received a rejection letter."

"Hmm," Tracy mused. "That might be true. When I was talking with Tawny, I noticed a list of topics written on Eric's personalized notepaper. It was there on her desk. He must have been asking for some resources on the Woman in White and some other incidents in Canton's history, like the stage line between Canton and Kirksville." She paused to take a sip of hot tea. "The Woman in White is why I went to see Tawny too. I was hoping she might have something about the incident in the archives, but she has less than we've got back at the office—or so she said. I'll need to venture into the nether regions to see what we have."

Annette arched her eyebrows. "Are you writing about that poor unidentified woman for your column? It's an odd topic to be researching at Christmastime. No, wait, as I recall, she died in December, right? During World War II?" When Tracy nodded, Annette added, "By the way, I really enjoyed the column you wrote a couple of weeks ago about the Hartley sisters and other elderly residents here in Canton. What did you call them? Living treasures? It was a good human-interest piece."

Tracy smiled her thanks. There was nothing a writer liked better than to hear someone praise her work. Yep. Words of praise. Definitely her love language. "Frankly, I'm not writing about the woman. My interest is personal." She went on to explain about her grandmother's scrapbook and what Aunt Ruth had said regarding Pearl's interest in identifying the unknown woman who'd arrived in Canton only to die alone and nameless a few days later.

Annette seemed intrigued. "I vaguely remember hearing about her. How no one ever came forward to identify her. Have you shown that scrapbook to Eric? If he is interested in the Woman in White, you could score some points by sharing what you know—what your grandmother knew. Especially if he's writing a book about the incident."

The Cameo Clue

Scowling, Tracy said, "I've thought about sharing it with him, but I'm not sure I want to now. I can't help wondering if he raked poor Tawny over the coals today too." She took another bite before adding, "I've got so much to do between now and Christmas Eve, but I can't get that poor young woman out of my mind." She sighed. "What I'd really like to do is sit down with someone here in Canton who had something to do with taking her to the hospital or maybe someone who was on the committee that offered to pay for her funeral expenses. Logically, I can assume that those individuals are all dead by now. But maybe there's a family member or two who are familiar with what happened."

"It's bewildering to think that no one—not a single person in Canton—ever came forward to identify her," Annette said. "After all, she bought a bus ticket to get here. She must have known someone in town. Not counting the Bermuda Triangle, it's just not possible to disappear off the face of the earth, right?"

"I know. It doesn't make sense," Tracy agreed.

Annette pointed her chopsticks at Tracy. "Anyway, if you want to speak with someone who has an indirect connection to the Woman in White, I might be able to help you."

Feeling a flutter of excitement, Tracy leaned forward. "Really?"

Annette nodded. "Her name is Elaine McLaren. She lives at Brookdale. She was just a kid back in 1944. She must be in her late eighties by now."

"Elaine McClary?" Tracy scrambled in her purse for a notepad and pen.

"No, McLaren."

"Do you think she'd have any clear memories of that day the woman arrived in Canton or the day she died? What's the connection?

Was she at the bus station when the woman arrived? Did she go to the cemetery to attend the burial?" Tracy arched an eyebrow.

"I'm not sure about any of that," Annette said, "but she surely has a story to tell. Elaine worked at the local floral shop for decades. She must know something about the white roses—the ones that someone kept putting on the grave each year around Christmastime. She might know who purchased those bouquets and why. That might provide you with a clue."

Tracy listened, intrigued. She silently thanked the Lord for this lead. Maybe Elaine would be able to provide some information that would help in solving Grandma Pearl's puzzle. "I'm definitely going to visit Elaine McLaren soon," she said. "Do you think she'd remember any pertinent details?"

Annette chuckled. "She's in a wheelchair, but her mind is sharp as a tack."

Tracy sat back. She was already considering whether she should take a poinsettia or a box of candy when she went to call on Elaine. "Do you think she would be willing to speak with me about the flowers? I don't want my questions to stir up any bad memories or anything like that."

"Elaine likes to talk," Annette assured her. "But you might want to take your grandmother's scrapbook along. Looking through it might help her remember."

"Good idea. I brought it to the office this morning to show you. It's on my desk," Tracy told her.

"You might want to visit the shop too, I think," Annette said. "I forget the name of it, but it's a couple of doors down from the hardware store."

The Cameo Clue

As they finished their lunch, Tracy's mind whirled with exciting possibilities. Elaine McLaren might hold the key to solving the mystery. She wondered if Grandma Pearl had ever approached someone at the floral shop to make inquiries about the white roses. She must have. Grandma Pearl had always been so painstakingly thorough about things, and she'd seemed very determined to not leave the young woman buried in the cemetery without a confirmed identity.

When the waitress placed their bill on the table, Tracy's cell phone gave a ping. Someone had sent her a text. She slipped her hand into the outside pocket of her purse to retrieve her phone. Surprisingly, the text was from Tawny, complete with a grinning emoji.

HEADS UP! YOUR GRUMPY BOSS IS ON HIS WAY BACK TO THE OFFICE.

Chapter Seven

*T*racy barely had time to slip off her jacket or tuck her purse into the bottom drawer of her desk before Eric stepped out of his office. He was tall and gangly with high cheekbones and a head full of dark hair. His face was stern. "Tracy." He frowned, his arms folded across his chest. "Could I see you in my office, please?"

She stopped short. Her cheeks grew warm. Tracy could almost feel the sympathetic looks from the rest of the staff. She dreaded a confrontation. It seemed so unnecessary.

Tracy scooped up the scrapbook and clutched it to her chest and made her way to Eric's office. Annette passed her coming out of the break room, with a muffin in one hand and a napkin in the other. They exchanged quick glances.

"Be brave, my lamb," Annette muttered.

Tracy gave a brisk nod. She refused to be intimidated. Mustering some self-control, she strode into Eric's office, hoping she appeared as cool as a cucumber. Eric sat down behind his desk with a huff. He didn't invite her to sit, so Tracy remained standing. She didn't close the door behind her. If Eric wanted this conversation to remain private, he could get up and shut the door himself.

"I couldn't help but notice that on your desk." His tone was accusatory as he tipped his chin forward, indicating the scrapbook.

The Cameo Clue

"And?" She kept her tone low, hoping she didn't sound intimidated. She felt rather breathless and a little trembly too. What was it about this kind of confrontation that made her feel so vulnerable?

"So what's up with that?" Eric snapped out the question.

Tracy felt a slight stirring of resentment. Why couldn't he admit he was interested in the topic? She figured he'd glanced through it already, wondering why she was interested in the same subject he was interested in. "I'm looking into an incident that took place in 1944—the death and burial of the Woman in White," she replied.

He didn't say anything at first, and Tracy wondered if he was ever going to ask her to sit down. He didn't. She remained standing, still clutching the scrapbook.

"I don't recall your mentioning it as one of your upcoming columns," Eric said, fixing her with a stare.

"I didn't. My interest is personal, but I may write something about it later on." She stared right back at him, refusing to be bullied. If she knew how to smooth his ruffled feathers, she'd make an attempt to do so. But how could she when she didn't even know what was wrong? Eric had been grumbling around the office like a bear with a sore head, as Grandpa Howard used to say. He was putting a serious damper on the holiday spirit of those working with him in the office.

Tracy knew he'd been divorced not so long ago. Could he be having trouble with his ex?

His elderly mother was ill. That was why he'd moved to Canton in the first place, to help his sisters take care of her. Perhaps Mrs. Watson was now more seriously ill than before. If he would only confide in someone, they might be able to help.

SECRETS FROM GRANDMA'S ATTIC

"It's really all about this," Tracy said, placing the scrapbook in the middle of his cluttered desk. "This is what sparked my interest. You ought to take a more thorough look."

Eric glared at her. "Where did you get it?"

"It belonged to my grandmother. It's nearly eighty years old, so be careful. The pages are brittle, and several of the articles have come unglued."

As he reached for the scrapbook, some of the intense color in his face faded. He appeared to be cooling down a little. She could only hope so. Eric turned the pages, frowning at each in turn.

Tracy went on. "Apparently, my grandmother had a keen interest in the incident. She was a young, unmarried woman at the time it occurred. She was close in age to the unidentified woman. Grandma Pearl sought to discover the dead woman's identity."

Without waiting to be asked, Tracy finally sat in the chair across from Eric's desk.

She noticed that he perused the pages quickly, not taking the time to read any of the articles or even the captions under the faded black-and-white newspaper photographs. Was he looking for something in particular? Tracy felt convinced that he'd already gone through it when she was having lunch with Annette.

"As you can see," she continued, "most of the clippings date back to 1944 and 1945. And then there are articles written years later—follow-up pieces and a few others observing the anniversary of the event."

Eric flapped a hand. "Have you read the articles in here?" He looked up at her searchingly.

Tracy nodded. "Yes, I've read all of them."

The Cameo Clue

"And your interest?"

"My neighbor Columbia Burke believes my grandmother wanted me to solve the mystery when I came to work for the newspaper. Grandma Pearl even said as much at one point to her. I'm trying to pick up where my grandmother left off."

Eric gave a snort as he closed the scrapbook and shoved it across the cluttered desk toward her. "If no one has identified the woman in nearly eighty years, what makes you think you can?"

Tracy studied his scowling face. Was there a note of derision in his tone? Or was it something else? He really didn't seem the least bit interested in the contents of the scrapbook, although he had let his gaze linger on the police sketch of the woman's face. What, then, was his interest in the subject? What aspect of the incident had captured his journalist's imagination? And was the Woman in White connected in some way to the other topics on the list he'd left with Tawny?

"I haven't started to do any research yet," Tracy told him. "For all I know, she's been identified and the matter is closed. It might not have made headlines, because the news about the incident was old, the news cold."

"Very cold," Eric said dryly, with a dismissive wave at the scrapbook. Then he turned away and reached for a file folder next to his computer.

That was that. The end of the matter. She had been dismissed. The fireworks she feared had fizzled out. She sent up a silent prayer of gratitude.

Tracy rose and scooped up the scrapbook, eager to return to her desk. However, she paused in the doorway of the office long enough to say, "Who knows? My investigation on Grandma Pearl's behalf may turn up something interesting enough for my Cantonbury Tales column."

"Whatever," Eric replied.

Tracy's eyebrows shot up. He was touchy. Very touchy. Was there something about the 1944 event that had him on edge? But what? And why? Tracy turned on her heel and left without saying another word. Returning to her desk, she put the scrapbook away in one of the lower drawers.

"What's eating him?" Jake hissed in a low voice. He paused beside Tracy's desk on his way back from the water cooler, thrusting his chin in the direction of Eric's office.

"Haven't a clue," Tracy said. She heaved another sigh.

"Even Scrooge was more cheerful," Jake muttered before returning to his own desk.

Jake had a point. Eric was way too grumpy. Tracy wondered if it would be worth trying to find out why. She wondered if she dared.

Annette came by her desk too. With a sharp tilt of her head, she indicated that Tracy should follow her to the break room. When they got there, Annette shut the door. "Okay, what's up? What did he say? Is he doing a story on Canton's mystery woman?" She stood there with her hands on her hips, looking hard at Tracy for answers.

"I honestly don't know," Tracy told her.

"But didn't you say you saw a list of topics he was researching at the historical society?"

Tracy nodded. "Yes, I saw a list on Tawny's desk."

"Any idea why Eric was there again today?"

"I'm assuming he went back to pick up any material Tawny might have discovered in their archives on those subjects. I'm hesitant to pump Tawny for information about it though," Tracy said. "We're friends, and I don't want to place her in a sticky situation."

"Did he look at your scrapbook?" Annette raised her eyebrows inquiringly and dropped her hands to her sides.

"Briefly. I got the impression he looked at it while we were at lunch too."

"He grew up in Quincy. It's not that far away," Annette pointed out. "There might be a family connection somewhere in the past to the Woman in White."

Tracy shrugged. Who could say?

"Watch out for skeletons in the closet," Annette warned. "When you go digging around in the past, you might find one hidden away somewhere. And it might be Eric's."

"I know," said Tracy. "But this is all so intriguing. I can hardly concentrate on anything else."

Annette said in a softer tone, "You're upset because the young woman fell through the cracks. There was no one to miss or mourn her."

"My grandma Pearl felt certain that no one *ever* falls through the cracks as far as God is concerned. The Lord sees everything, knows everything."

"Your grandmother must have been a wise woman." Annette smiled.

"Indeed she was."

Annette opened the break room door. "We'd better get back to work before Eric finds us in here. He'll probably guess what we've been talking about and get his knickers in a twist all over again!"

July 14, 1944
Oaklawn Retreat
Jacksonville, Illinois

Dear Aunt Violet and Uncle Alfred,

As you can see from the return address on the envelope, I'm no longer living at Mrs. Batterson's boardinghouse. I'm in a TB sanatorium! Can you believe it? The doctors say I have tuberculosis. I didn't want to come. I don't have the money to pay. I'm not asking you for money though, so don't worry. Dr. Henderson says my medical expenses will be paid for by the county's indigent fund. Tom would be so ashamed to know I'm considered indigent. He believed in hard work and paying our own way. Although I miss him terribly, I'm so glad he's not alive to see me in these circumstances.

Because I kept coughing up blood, the doctor ordered that X-ray like he said he would. It was an interesting experience. It didn't hurt a bit. Apparently, I have lesions on my lungs. TB is contagious, so I can't stay in the boardinghouse with Jilly and the others. I'm supposed to have complete bed rest too. I cried a little when they told me I'll be here in the sanatorium for six to nine months, depending on how I respond to treatment. Everyone calls it "the san" for short. You can write to me here. You will write, won't you?

When doctors say, "complete bed rest," they really mean it. I can get up to use the toilet, but that is all. They are very rigid about their rules. I can't really do anything but stay in bed, propped up by bunches of pillows. I can't even take deep breaths. I'm supposed to breathe slow and shallow. I'm leading the life of a log! I lie here mindful of the whirring sound of the fan blades as they spin the warm air around the ward, hardly cooling it down at all. But it's better than nothing. Perspiration causes my pajamas to stick to me. Sometimes they give me a cold compress for the back of my neck when I'm running a temperature, which is most of the time now. Having a low-grade fever all the time is one of the signs of TB. Did you know that?

They say all I need is complete rest, lots of fresh air, and nourishing food, and I'll be cured—eventually. But they can't tell me exactly when that will be. Weeks? Months? The nurses are nice enough, but some of the other women in my ward are real gripers, always complaining about everything—the food, the boredom, the heat. I'm determined to be cheerful. Jilly reminded me of that before I left Peoria. "Keep your chin up," she said. "Be cheerful." I do try. Isn't there a Bible verse about cheerfulness being good medicine or something like that?

The san is huge and is located on a hill at the edge of town. Looks like a castle to me. Some of the patients call it a "lung resort." I'm in a ward with a dozen other women.

Patients with money can pay for a private room. My bed is comfortable enough. Thank goodness, since the majority of my time is spent in it. The sheets are—how shall I put it—rough and sturdy. One woman who has a private room brought her own satin sheets from home. The nurses had them fumigated before putting them on her bed!

I have a bedside table with a hook on the edge. The nurses hang a little bag there for me to put my soiled tissues in. There's also a little wax cup to hold my sputum when I cough it up. The nurses collect these things and burn them in the incinerator in the cellar each day. Even though we are supposed to be resting all day long, they get us up at the crack of dawn to use the toilet and wash up a little, and then they take our temperature. They do that four times a day!

Can you imagine? It's a bit of a trial, I can tell you.

It's bad news to have a fever, no matter how slight. It means the bacteria is still active in my body. They write everything down on a chart chained to the foot of my bed. It's wearisome. And my chest hurts a lot. It feels like a tight fist clenched inside there. The pain wears me out. Sometimes I can hardly breathe, which I suppose is a good thing, since they don't want me to take deep breaths anyway.

The woman in the bed next to mine is named Nora Fickett. She's married and has three kids. Can you imagine having to be in the san while your kids are at home without you? Nora talks about them all the time. When she's upset or surprised about something she says, "Oh my stars and garters!" Isn't that funny?

Her kids and husband can come visit sometimes on Sundays. There's a parlor downstairs for that. Nora is on the mend, so she gets privileges, like being able to leave her bed to go to the parlor. She's been here three months already.

Here in the san, it's lights out at nine. After sleeping all day, it's sometimes hard for me and the other women in the ward to go to sleep again so early at night. Some ladies sneak and read a book under the covers. Others whisper to patients in the beds next to them. Even when I'm bone tired and want to sleep, sometimes it's hard to do because, after all, with a dozen women in the ward, it's never completely quiet. We've got those who snore. What a racket! One woman on the opposite side of the room whistles when she snores. It's like a high-pitched squeal. There's lots of sighing in the dark too, and some heavy breathers and the ones who have occasional nightmares. But the ones who cry for their families and children are the hardest to listen to.

I asked the nurse this morning whether tuberculosis is hereditary. She says definitely not. I was worried that you or Dory might come down with it if it was. Or even Uncle Alfred, although he's not my blood kin. I also asked the nurse if I could have children one day if I ever remarry, which is not something I think about much. I'm still missing Tom and don't suppose I'll ever love another man the way I loved him.

The nurse said yes, I could have a baby one day, but I won't be able to nurse. I'll have to use a bottle.

When I'm not resting and lying around like a log, I'm eating. They feed us so much, I can't believe there's rationing going on. We get eggs every day for breakfast and lots of milk and hot cocoa. So much milk! We had split pea soup and saltines for lunch—and that was just for starters. Then came baked fish with lots of vegetables, including pickled onions. Never had one of those before, but I liked them.

There's always bread and butter. Real butter too, not that oleomargarine. And guess what? For dessert, we had ice cream sundaes with chocolate sauce. Last night we had baked apples, which I love. Lots of brown sugar. Yummy! I do miss Mrs. Batterson's fried chicken though. We never get fried anything here.

Some of the patients grumble about the food. I wouldn't dare. I mean, someone is footing the bill, and I'm eating for free. I'm grateful. I really am. We even get fresh strawberries from a nearby farm. And once, they served them on a dish with a little scoop of powdered sugar. The nurse called it "strawberries in the snow." Isn't that something?

I eat in bed on a tray. But the patients who don't have fevers can eat in the dining hall. It's very elegant with wood paneling and chandeliers. I'm trying to build up my strength so I can eat in there one day. They say that gaining weight is a sign of recovery, and so I'm trying to eat, but I still don't have much of an appetite. When I walk to the bathroom, I feel shaky, and my heart beats like mad. I get very breathless if I use my arms too much or bend down. It's worrisome. But I'm determined to beat this illness.

Last Wednesday I apparently moved around too much and became very exhausted. Also, I had a queer little pain in my chest which wouldn't go away and a rise in my temperature, so they sent the doctor to me. He said he thought it had nothing to do with my lungs, but I'm to stay in bed till my temperature settles down.

One of the nurses told me that malnutrition is a cause of tuberculosis. Her name is Fanny Booth. I must call her Nurse Booth, but the other women on the ward sometimes teasingly call her Nurse Fanny. She's a spinster with small metal spectacles and a cloud of salt-and-pepper hair arranged on top of her head in a tight bun. I've never been malnourished in my life! And I told her so.

She also said TB afflicts "poor people" who live in crowded, poorly ventilated conditions. I said "Phooey!" We never lived like that—not when I was with my folks nor with Tom either. I must have caught it on the bus or the train or somewhere when sitting next to a sick person. They say it's highly contagious. So it wouldn't matter if you lived in the cleanest mansion with huge airy windows and ate the healthiest, most expensive food in town. If you are exposed to someone with TB, you can get infected.

I hope you'll write to me soon. Will you? I'm allowed to read letters and books. They have a small library here, but I can't go down yet. A nurse will bring me a book if I want one, but really, I'm so tired, I sleep most of the time. Weary to the bone. I'm trying not to fret about things. Am trying to obey all the rigid rules too. Some patients can't handle it, and they leave against doctors' orders. And if anyone gets caught spitting on the floor, it's an automatic discharge. Out they go! But who would be so crude as to spit on the floor, I ask you?

I must finish this letter now. I've been working on it for days. Who knew writing could be so exhausting? A nurse will be coming soon to take me outside to the screened porch for more fresh air. They push me in a wheelchair and leave me there to take short, shallow breaths. The grounds are real pretty with the flowers and shrubs in bloom. If you listen, you can hear the birds twittering in the trees. I feel blessed to be recuperating in such pleasant surroundings. They don't let us sit close to other patients though. They don't want us chatting and laughing and such. We're supposed to be still and rest and listen to the birds.

Sometimes I feel guilty thinking about Mrs. B and my friends at the boardinghouse. They are all working hard in the factories and doing war work—rolling bandages, knitting socks for the troops and such in the evenings. And here I sit doing nothing. Oh my stars and garters! I'm just like a log.

Your worthless niece,

Trula

P.S. Please write.

Chapter Eight

When his order was placed before him, a look of satisfaction softened Jeff's gray eyes. "I love biscuits and gravy," he declared, tucking in.

Tracy took a bite of her cheese omelet. "I love eating breakfast out on a weekday," she said. "It makes me feel like we're on vacation or like we're celebrating something. You can treat me to breakfast at PJ's anytime." She glanced around the bustling diner with its battered wooden tables and booths. It was homey. She liked it here. Glittering garland graced the walls, and Christmas tunes could be heard above the usual din. When Robert West, sitting on his usual stool, looked up from reading the newspaper to give her a nod, she raised a hand and smiled.

"Hey, it's the least I can do for my favorite girl, especially when she's kind enough to give me a ride to work," Jeff said. His car was in the shop getting an oil change and the tires rotated. "Besides, we are celebrating something, aren't we? It's a Tuesday, and from the looks of the sky, it just might snow. 'This is the day that the Lord has made. We shall rejoice and be glad in it.' That's one of Pastor Gary's favorite Bible verses."

"Mine too," Tracy said. "If you can't get a ride home later, give me a call. I have Jana's piano lesson this afternoon, but I can come get you afterwards."

"Don't worry about it," Jeff told her. "I'm sure I can catch a ride with someone."

After taking another bite of her breakfast followed by a sip of orange juice, Tracy said, "Speaking of Pastor Gary, do you think he would know anything about the mystery woman?"

Last night, she'd told Jeff about her dodging Eric Watson at the historical society and the conversation that had followed in Eric's office. Jeff had frowned and told her not to let Eric's rudeness ruin her holiday spirit. Tracy had taken his advice.

Instead of fretting over Eric's behavior, she'd spent the evening with Jeff, finishing up their Christmas gift list to make sure they weren't leaving anyone out. They had purchased presents for their own grown children and their spouses, the grandbabies—including Anna and Chad's newborn daughter, Elizabeth Pearl—and Amy and her youngsters. They still had to purchase something for Miles, Natalie, and Colton.

When she'd told Jeff about buying socks and underwear for Matt and Jana, Jeff had chortled. "Oh, sure, they'll love that."

Now, as she bit into a piece of sourdough toast, she felt relieved that she didn't have to worry about a present for Amy's bridal shower tomorrow—the one hosted by her colleagues at the school. During the summer, Tracy had purchased a handmade maple rocking chair with a cane bottom at the Amish fair. Amy had always wanted one. Tracy had considered giving it to her for Christmas, but then she decided to give it to her as a bridal gift instead. Aunt Ruth had promised to watch the kids after classes were dismissed so Amy could enjoy the after-school shower being given in her honor.

"So, do you think Pastor Gary would know anything?" Tracy repeated. The incident had taken place long before he was born, but Pastor Gary was a Canton native. He might have heard rumors and gossip about the Woman in White. He certainly would have had relatives living in Canton at the time. Over the years, he might have overheard snatches of family conversation on the subject. Maybe they'd even told him something about what had occurred back then.

"I wouldn't be surprised," Jeff replied. "Your grandmother took Pastor Gary into her confidence many times. They were close. She might have told him something about the incident she didn't share with Columbia."

Tracy took another sip of orange juice.

"You spent a lot of time online last night," Jeff noted. "I noticed you went through the scrapbook again too. Were you looking for something in particular?"

"Yes," Tracy said. "I wanted to see how many newspaper articles about the Woman in White I could find online. Stories that are different than the ones in the scrapbook. I found an article with a brief interview of the doctor who treated the woman when she died, one with a few quotes from the minister who performed the funeral, and an interview of a town council member."

"Any possible leads to pursue for further information?" Jeff asked, reaching for his coffee mug.

With a wave of her fork, Tracy replied, "I'm not sure. Those individuals have passed away, but they may have descendants or elderly relatives still living here in Canton who might be able to answer some of my questions." Having finished her breakfast, Tracy placed her fork on her plate. She sighed. It wasn't going to be easy finding out new information about a Jane Doe who died nearly eighty years ago.

"Call Dale. He might dig up something useful in the old police files," Jeff suggested.

Tracy straightened. "Great idea."

Police Sergeant Dale Leewright was a good friend and certainly would have access to anything the police might have in their files—if they kept information about something that had happened decades ago. As Eric had pointed out yesterday, it was a very cold case. Very.

Thinking of the police sketch that had been circulated in the newspapers long ago, Tracy mused, "The woman was young. She had the finely chiseled features of an old-fashioned Gibson girl. Do you know what I mean?"

Jeff chuckled. "Yes, sweetie, I know exactly what you mean. I'm a history professor, remember? I know a little about Charles Dana Gibson and the illustrations he drew of young American women prior to World War I."

Tracy grinned. "Show-off. Of course you'd know. Anyway, there's a good sketch of the cameo in the paper too. I'm sure the one Grandma Pearl pinned in the scrapbook is the same one. If not, it's certainly identical. I'm going to have to find out how she came to be in possession of it. In the sketch, it's pinned to the woman's dress. It could be a clue to her identity. As you said before, it's probably a family heirloom."

As Tracy drained the last of her orange juice, Jeff surprised her by saying, "Why don't we go out to the cemetery and look at the grave now? It shouldn't take long, if we can find it."

SECRETS FROM GRANDMA'S ATTIC

Her heart gave a sudden thud against her rib cage. "I'd love to do that. I've even been thinking about it." She much preferred going with Jeff than going alone. Cemeteries were sad places. At least, she found them so. Going with her husband would make it seem more of an adventure than a chore. "Are you sure you don't mind? Won't you be late for your Tuesday faculty meeting?"

Jeff shook his head. "It's been postponed until after the semester is officially over. Everyone's busy with finals and turning in grades on time, that sort of thing. Let me pay the bill, and then we'll go."

Tracy didn't have to be asked twice. She scrambled into her coat and scarf while Jeff paid for their meal. Soon they were driving to the edge of town to Oak Grove Cemetery. She'd always wondered why the place had been given that name. As far as she could tell, there were no oaks. Certainly, there were plenty of other trees, mainly evergreens of one sort or another, but no oaks. Maybe there had been an oak or two back in the day.

Before they reached their destination, Tracy gave Annette a quick call.

"On another hot lead?" Annette asked.

Tracy snorted. "No, Jeff and I are headed to the cemetery."

"The Woman in White again?" Annette whispered.

"Yes," Tracy whispered back. She noticed Jeff's glance and gave him a wink.

"All right, see you when you get here," Annette said cheerfully. "I want to hear all about it."

Despite the overcast sky and feeble sunshine, the cemetery appeared rather colorful with small American flags left over from Veterans' Day observances, a wide array of fake flowers, and a few

Christmas wreaths dotting graves here and there. They found a place to park and got out of the car. It was quiet. Peaceful. Even the finches and sparrows twittered in subdued tones. The gravestones appeared to be hunkered down for the winter. When they passed a grave with a bright pink teddy bear propped against the stone, Tracy could feel a lump lodge in her throat.

At one point, she couldn't shake the feeling that they were being watched. Was it possible that Eric was checking up on her? Tracy turned her head sharply. No one was there.

In fact, there was no one else in sight. She lengthened her stride to keep up with Jeff.

"Do you know where the grave is?" Jeff asked, breaking the hushed silence. The crunching of gravel beneath their feet sounded unnaturally loud.

"She died in 1944," Tracy answered. "I'm assuming she'll be in that right-hand corner." She pointed. Many of the town's citizens who'd died during the war years had been buried there. So it was not quite like hunting for a needle in a haystack. She pulled the collar of her coat up around her ears, scrunched her shoulders, and followed Jeff to that corner of the cemetery.

Her hunch proved to be correct. They quickly found the simple, white marble headstone. It was rectangular in shape and inscribed with the words, THE WOMAN IN WHITE, DIED DECEMBER 21, 1944. There were no white roses to brighten up the grave. That certainly made sense. The person or persons who'd originally honored the woman buried here had surely passed away too.

"No white roses," Jeff noted as though he'd read her mind.

"No white roses," Tracy repeated.

SECRETS FROM GRANDMA'S ATTIC

Something rustled in the brambles. There was a crack of a twig. Suddenly, Tracy could hear her own heart beating in her ears. She reached for Jeff's arm and clung to it. She was being silly. This had to stop. She'd watched far too many creepy movies with cemetery scenes. With her other hand, she took her phone from her coat pocket and snapped a couple of photos of the old tombstone.

"The roses might be an angle you could pursue though," Jeff went on. He seemed unmindful of any spooky atmosphere. "Back then you couldn't walk into a supermarket and buy a bouquet of white roses. At least I don't think you could. In fact, I'm not so sure it would be that easy to buy white roses from a small floral shop. They'd have to place a special order, wouldn't you think? White roses aren't all that common, are they?"

Tracy hadn't thought of that. "You're probably right. Annette suggested I visit the florist shop here in town. Maybe they've kept sales records from the past." It was possible, but Tracy seriously doubted it.

Jeff went on. "And I'll bet whoever bought the flowers paid in cash. They didn't have credit cards in 1944. In fact, the first credit cards didn't really make it onto the scene until the late 1950s."

"The person who purchased the roses may have had a charge account with the shop though," Tracy suggested. An account with a name and local address.

Perhaps.

She hoped so.

Nodding, Jeff agreed with that possibility. "On the other hand, anyone charging flowers to their account wouldn't remain anonymous for long."

True.

"But why white roses?" Tracy pondered aloud. "There must be a significance to the color." Respect? Grief? Purity? "There's some sort of language of flowers, I know, but I'm not familiar with the specifics."

"I'm sure the florist could tell you."

"I can certainly ask. Or I can look it up." Tracy took a deep breath. The air was crisp and sharp with cold.

"Seems like a romantic gesture, if you ask me." Jeff shoved his ungloved hands deep into his coat pockets. He stared down at the stone. "Maybe the woman came to Canton to meet her fiancé? A husband?"

Tracy shook her head. "I doubt it. If that was true, why wouldn't he identify her after the sketch appeared in the paper?" Then a different, rather unsavory thought occurred to her. "Maybe she came to town to meet her lover. Perhaps he was a married man, and that's why he never came forward to give her a name."

Jeff picked up the thread of the idea, conjecturing, "Okay, they said she suffered from tuberculosis. She was sick. Maybe she knew she was dying and wanted to see the man one last time before the end."

Tracy arched an eyebrow. "That's plausible."

"Who else can you interview about the incident?" Jeff probed.

"There are several old photographs of the minister, the doctor, and some of the members of the benevolence committee that agreed to pay for this." She gestured to the headstone. "I'm sure they've all passed away, but one or more of them might have relatives still living in Canton. I could track them down and speak with them. If

SECRETS FROM GRANDMA'S ATTIC

they are as sprightly as the Hartley sisters, they might be able to provide me with a clue or two."

"And don't forget Pastor Gary," Jeff reminded her.

"I won't." Tracy shivered. "Let's go. It's cold out here."

As they made their way back to the car, Jeff took Tracy by the elbow. "Listen, sweetie, you might want to step lightly as you dig into this. Columbia is right—you could be exposing skeletons in someone's closet, and that could be... unpleasant. Please be careful. Someone might want to keep the family secret in the family."

Tracy glanced nervously over both shoulders and accepted the warning.

Chapter Nine

Tracy, I want you to revise that article you did last week on Christmas activities sponsored by the various churches and civic organizations in town. Remove those programs that have already taken place—like that breakfast with Santa that was held on Saturday—and add anything that might have been omitted in the first piece. We'll run it in tomorrow's edition."

Eric stood beside her desk. He let his gaze sweep across it several times as though taking note of what she'd been working on. Tracy followed his gaze. Was he looking for something in particular? Like what? The scrapbook maybe? It was safe at home on her dresser.

"I'll get right on it," Tracy assured him. Having just learned from a reliable source that the American Heritage Girls would be holding a bake sale in the bank lobby next week, she would make a point of listing that bit of news first. She felt sure they'd appreciate the free publicity.

Eric gave her a curt nod. "Add two or three photos. Something festive and seasonal. A manger scene or something."

"On it, Chief," she quipped. She looked up from her keyboard and smiled.

Frowning, Eric walked away but not before letting his gaze run over her desk again.

Tracy watched his retreating figure. Still grumpy, it seemed. Eric paused at the water cooler and then made his way to Bethany's desk to speak with her. Something was surely wrong at home or with his extended family. Tracy wondered how she could find out without prying. She and Eric weren't close. Colleagues, yes, but not really friends.

She remembered that Pastor Gary had once told their Bible study group that December was often a busy month for ministers because of suicides, marriage breakups, and other problems in the community. Many people felt blue during the holiday season, he'd told them. Not everyone enjoyed a happy, Norman Rockwell-picture-perfect Christmas. Tracy silently lifted Eric and his family in prayer, feeling helpless to do anything else.

Retrieving her purse from the bottom drawer of her desk, Tracy made up her mind to visit Pastor Gary right now. She'd been looking for a reason to do so, and Eric had just given her one. She could kill two birds with one stone, as Grandpa Howard used to say. She would take a photo of the impressive poinsettia display in the church foyer to go with the Christmas events article and talk with Pastor Gary about the Woman in White.

She found the minister emerging from his vehicle in the church parking lot when she pulled in. He wore a heavy brown leather coat that reminded her of a pilot's flight jacket and carried a bag from the local sub sandwich shop.

"You're just the man I want to see," she called out to him, waving.

He raised the bag. "I'm having lunch. Have you had yours?"

Tracy shook her head. "Had a huge breakfast at PJ's with Jeff this morning. I won't need to eat for days."

Pastor Gary chuckled as he held the door open for her. "Is this a personal visit, or a professional one? We didn't have an appointment, did we?"

"It's both, actually, and if you're busy, I can come back," Tracy assured him.

"No, it's fine, if you don't mind that I eat while we talk." He led the way to his office. Maureen, the church secretary, wasn't in. Tracy assumed she was on her lunch hour too. "I have some hospital visits to make this afternoon and need to keep up my strength." He gave her a half smile as he removed his sandwich from the bag.

"I need to take a photo of the display in the foyer for the newspaper," Tracy informed him. "But I also want to talk to you about something that happened a long time ago. About the unidentified woman who is buried out at the Oak Grove Cemetery."

Pastor Gary raised an eyebrow. "Yes, the mysterious young woman who arrived by bus and died shortly before Christmas, as I recall. Of course, that was all before my time, but my parents, aunts, and uncles talked about the incident. I think they referred to her as the Woman in White. When I was a teenager, I had friends who would venture out at night during the month of December, hoping to catch someone placing a bouquet of white roses on the grave. That was the part of the mystery that intrigued me the most. Those roses. Who placed them there year after year?"

Tracy's cheeks flushed with excitement. "Yes, that intrigues me too. I want to know if Grandma Pearl ever talked to you about the incident." She went on to hastily explain about the scrapbook and the cameo brooch while he ate his lunch.

SECRETS FROM GRANDMA'S ATTIC

"As a matter of fact, your grandmother and I did have a conversation once about that young woman." Pastor Gary settled back in his chair, placing a paper napkin across his lap. He took another bite of his sandwich.

Tracy waited patiently for him to finish chewing before asking, "What did my grandmother say? Did she ever mention the scrapbook or show it to you? I want to know why the incident interested her so much. Jeff and I went to the cemetery this morning to look at the grave. There weren't any white roses there, I might add."

"No, that custom has fallen by the wayside, or so I've been told." He swiped a bit of mayonnaise from his chin with a napkin. "Whoever started that has surely passed away." He glanced up at the ceiling. "Let me see, it's been what? Seventy-five or eighty years ago, right?"

Tracy nodded. "It was 1944."

"But how can I help you? I probably don't know any more about the incident than you do." He regarded her with a puzzled frown.

"You said Grandma Pearl talked to you about the woman years ago. I want to know why she brought it up and what she said," Tracy explained. "Besides, you grew up here in Canton. You might know someone who was involved in some way with the mysterious lady. I've already talked to my aunt Ruth. She didn't know anything. I'm guessing my aunt Abigail doesn't either."

"All I know is that your grandmother served on the benevolence committee that decided to provide a headstone for her grave."

Tracy felt a twinge of disappointment. Columbia had already said as much. She'd hoped Pastor Gary would have something new to share.

The Cameo Clue

"My grandmother served on that same committee," Pastor Gary told her. "The women wanted a brief memorial service by the graveside. They believed no one should die alone and unmourned. Following the interment there was a small luncheon at the office of one of the county councillors."

"It's a very nice headstone," Tracy said.

Pastor Gary nodded. "Your grandmother and the others on the committee insisted. Just in case a family member should show up later, they wanted to show that Canton residents were not slack in their kindness to a stranger."

"I was expecting something..." She paused, searching for the right word.

"Something cheaper?" Pastor Gary arched his eyebrows.

Tracy could feel herself blushing. It was true. Before she'd seen the picture of the headstone in the scrapbook, she had expected one of those simple metal plates sunk into the ground, not a nice headstone neatly carved and in good taste. Something relatives would want for a beloved family member.

"As I said, your grandmother was a very sensitive young woman. She wanted the bereaved, should they ever arrive in Canton looking for their missing loved one, to see that she'd been buried with consideration and respect." Emotion deepened his glance. Not sadness exactly, but something more sentimental. He had been close with Grandma Pearl. "I miss her," he said.

Tracy said simply, "Me too."

After taking another bite of his sandwich, Pastor Gary went on. "The minister at the time was a man named Harvey Edge. A good and faithful man by all accounts. I never knew him. He too was quite distressed by the young woman's death. And even more so as the weeks and months passed without anyone stepping forward to identify her."

"How do you know?" Tracy asked, frowning.

"Your grandmother told me."

"Do you know if Pastor Edge had any family left in Canton? Someone I could speak to about the burial ceremony?" Tracy asked.

"None that I'm aware of. He wasn't from here originally. Came down from Michigan, I think. Why your interest in this, Tracy? Are you writing about it in your column?"

"No, I'm not writing an article. It's personal. Ever since I found the scrapbook and realized that it meant something to my grandmother, I feel like I should do something."

"After all this time?" He arched an eyebrow. "And what do you think you can do, exactly? Seems like a futile pursuit to me."

"Perhaps, but Columbia told me that the incident bothered my grandmother for years. That at one time she'd even considered asking me to investigate the matter. I suppose Grandma thought I'd have access to a wider selection of resources once I joined the newspaper staff."

"But she never talked to you about it?"

"Never."

Maybe Pastor Gary was right. It was rather futile after nearly eighty years had passed. But she couldn't help but feel that putting the unsolved mystery to rest would be one way to honor her grandmother's life.

"Pearl showed me the scrapbook once," Gary went on. "She'd pinned the cameo pin inside, as I recall."

The Cameo Clue

Leaning forward, Tracy asked, "So, it did belong to the dead woman? How did my grandmother come to have possession of it?"

"Pastor Edge believed someone might be able to identify the brooch and subsequently identify the woman, and Pearl volunteered to hang on to it. They wondered if she might have been hospitalized before coming to Canton, so they sent copies of the police sketch to area hospitals, hoping someone would recognize her and contact the church."

"The articles mentioned she'd suffered from tuberculosis, but I think the cause of death was listed as pneumonia," Tracy said.

"The white plague. That's what my grandmother called TB." Pastor Gary wiped his hands on a napkin and set aside the remains of his meal.

"I've never heard it called that," Tracy said. "I thought it was called consumption."

"That too," Pastor Gary acknowledged. "It was deadly and highly contagious. Treatment is much better now. People don't have to go away to a sanatorium for months at a time."

At that moment, Maureen Dalton, the church secretary, popped her head into the office. She had brown hair and glasses and wore a green turtleneck sweater with a cluster of holly embroidered in the middle. "Pastor, I'm back! Oh, hi Tracy."

Tracy raised a hand in greeting. "Hi, Maureen. I like your sweater."

Maureen acknowledged the compliment with an even brighter smile and then returned to her desk in the outer office. Tracy rose to take her leave. "Thanks for your help, Pastor Gary."

SECRETS FROM GRANDMA'S ATTIC

"I'm afraid I haven't been much help at all." He gave her a wan smile.

"But you have. Until just now, I wasn't certain that the cameo belonged to the dead woman."

"It appeared to be a family heirloom," Pastor Gary said. "Pearl felt certain that someone someday might be able to identify it and then they might be able to give the poor woman a name."

"By chance do you know if they buried the woman in her white coat and dress? The outfit she was wearing when she came to town?" Tracy asked.

"Pearl said they took a clean dress from the woman's suitcase and buried her in that. They had the white dress and coat cleaned and placed in the suitcase. They felt the traveling outfit she arrived in might help identify her later on."

Tracy's heart skipped a beat. "Suitcase? The woman had a suitcase?"

Pastor Gary chuckled. "She would hardly be traveling with saddlebags, now would she?"

"Of course not." Tracy dropped back down into the chair. "Please, *please* tell me you know what happened to that suitcase!"

Chapter Ten

The suitcase. Where is it?" Tracy resisted the urge to hold her breath.

Pastor Gary shrugged. "I don't know. I believe at one time your grandmother said it had been taken into police custody." He chuckled as though pleased by the weak joke.

"That makes sense," Tracy said with a nod. She made another mental note to call Sergeant Dale Leewright, as Jeff had suggested earlier. Maybe Dale could help track it down—if it was still around. "The contents might provide a clue."

"Don't count on it," her pastor told her. "They may have donated everything to the homeless shelter or one of the local charity thrift shops when no one stepped forward to put in a claim."

Tracy silently acknowledged this could be true. Besides, was it likely she'd find anything after nearly eighty years had passed? Hadn't everyone in the previous decades had the opportunity to rummage through the suitcase searching for clues to the woman's identity? Nevertheless, Tracy wanted to look for herself.

After thanking Pastor Gary for his help and promising to keep him informed of her progress, Tracy said goodbye to him and Maureen and then paused in the foyer to take a few quick photos of the elaborate poinsettia display. She then drove to the Baptist church across town which had an attractive outdoor nativity scene on the front lawn and took photos of that too.

Back at the office, she typed up the revised article, downloaded the photos, and emailed everything to Annette for editing. Although still comfortably full after her enormous breakfast at PJ's, she couldn't resist the star-shaped sugar cookies she discovered in the break room and helped herself to one, along with a fresh cup of coffee.

She was about to call Dale at the police station when her cell phone gave a *ping*. It was from Amy, short and sweet. CALL ME.

Tracy glanced at the clock on the wall. School was still in session. It was unusual for Amy to call during work hours. Tracy hoped nothing was wrong. She realized her pulse had quickened.

Amy answered immediately. "Thanks for getting back to me so quickly, Tracy."

"Everything okay? Aren't you in class with the kids?"

"They're in the gym for PE," Amy replied. After a slight pause, she added, "I need a favor."

"Sure. What can I do?" Tracy could feel a frown pinching her forehead. Something was up. She could hear the tightness in Amy's voice.

"It's Jana. She was sent to the principal's office today—and not for the first time this month."

"What!" Tracy had a hard time imagining her young niece doing anything so bad that she'd have to be reprimanded by the school principal. "What happened?"

"She got in a fight during morning recess—yelling and name-calling." Amy let out a shudder of a sigh. "She actually told Natalie she didn't want to be friends with her anymore."

For a moment, Tracy was speechless. Jana was a sweet, bubbly child. And besides, Miles's daughter was Jana's best friend and had been for quite some time. Tracy could hardly believe that Jana would behave in such a way with anyone, much less Natalie. And she said so.

"I know," Amy said. "They've been so close. But that's not the only thing. Jana has been…I don't know…different lately. She's been quiet and rather sullen. She won't tell me why. You've raised two kids. Is this a phase or something, like the terrible twos? Do eight-year-olds go through phases like this?"

"No, I don't think I've ever heard of the Angry Eights," Tracy said. "But that's not like Jana. She's a warmhearted, good-natured child."

"Normally, yes. But she was surprisingly rude to Miles when he stopped by the other evening. And that book of fairy tales he gave her for her birthday, I found it in the trash the other day. She'd scribbled all over the cover with a black marker. I don't know what's going on. Would you talk to her and try to find out? She won't talk to me. I've tried, and she either pouts and clams up or she bursts into tears."

"You want me to find out what's going on with her?"

"Would you? Could you?" Amy sounded desperate.

Tracy took a deep breath. Being a parent was difficult. Without sacrificial love, prayer, and patience, she didn't know how people got the job done. "I'll try. But I don't know if she'll confide in me."

"Maybe you could spend a little extra time with her when you come over for her piano lesson," Amy suggested.

"Yes, I'll have a word with her. I have parenting experience, but I'm not an expert, you know." Tracy hoped Amy wasn't expecting a miracle. "Kids are complex," she added by way of warning. "Sometimes they say one thing but really mean something else."

Amy exclaimed in an exasperated tone, "You're telling me!"

They spoke for a few moments longer, with Tracy giving her sister a few words of encouragement. After the call, she sat for some time staring at the far wall, going over in her mind various ways to approach Jana later that afternoon. What a week this was turning out to be. First, she had to deal with a prickly editor and now an angry, out of control young niece. Wasn't this supposed to be the season of peace and goodwill? Tracy tried to imagine what Natalie had done to provoke such behavior from Jana. She said a silent prayer that the Lord would guide her in the conversation and give her just the right words to speak.

Tracy had promised to be at Amy's promptly at four o'clock that afternoon. She wanted to help Amy, of course. But she didn't want to jeopardize her friendship with Jana. She loved the little girl and had enjoyed their piano lessons. She treasured their time together each week and wanted to keep nurturing their growing relationship.

Putting that problem aside for the moment, Tracy reached for her cell phone to call Dale Leewright and ask for his help. Tracy had Dale's personal cell number but decided not to use it. She was calling about official business and felt it should go through the proper channels. She tapped out the nonemergency number for the police station and asked for Dale's extension. He answered promptly and sounded pleased when he discovered that it was Tracy calling.

"Hey there, Tracy! Merry Christmas. What are you up to? On the trail of an intriguing story? Do you have another secret tunnel you want me to explore?"

Tracy laughed, recalling the excitement of discovering the tunnel underneath the Hartley mansion that led to the river—a tunnel used back in the bootlegging days. "Nothing quite that exciting, but a little mysterious maybe."

"I'm intrigued already," Dale said.

Tracy detected a note of humor in his tone. "I'm trying to track down an old suitcase that might be in police custody."

Dale laughed. "A suitcase in police custody? You're pulling my leg."

"I mean it might have been logged in somewhere as evidence, about eighty years ago."

"Wow, that's going back a while. What was the crime?"

"It wasn't a crime, exactly," Tracy said. "I'm looking into the unsolved mystery of the Woman in White."

"Hmm, sounds vaguely familiar," Dale replied.

Tracy gave him a brief account of the young woman's arrival in Canton and subsequent death. "Can you chase down her suitcase for me?" Tracy resisted the urge to cross her fingers.

There was a pause before Dale said, "When did this happen? How long ago?"

Tracy chuckled. "Maybe I should begin at the beginning."

"Good idea," he agreed. "I'm listening."

Knowing she had his full attention, Tracy launched into the familiar recitation about the scrapbook and the 1944 incident that had prompted Grandma Pearl's interest all those years ago. She also added the information she'd received from Pastor Gary concerning the suitcase.

When she finished, Dale asked, "Can you give me a description of the...er...culprit? The missing suitcase, I mean."

"I have no idea what it looks like, but you can't have that many suitcases stashed away in your evidence locker, right?"

"Technically, it's not evidence. At least not evidence of a crime," Dale said. "According to the newspaper articles you've mentioned, the woman died of natural causes. The only crime seems to be that no one stepped forward to claim her. And technically, even that isn't a crime. Sad and shameful perhaps, but not criminal."

Tracy leaned forward, resting one elbow on her desk. "But could you please look around the station and see if the suitcase is there? I know the incident took place before you and I were even born, but maybe you know somebody who knows somebody. You know how that goes. They might know where it can be found."

"Sure, I'll look into it, Tracy, but I can't guarantee I'll come up with anything. After all, eighty years is a long, long time ago."

Tracy silently acknowledged the truth of this.

"You said Pastor Gary told you the police took the suitcase?" Dale probed.

"Yes, my grandmother told him so."

"Okay, I'll see what I can scrounge up. But like I said, I can't guarantee I'll find the suitcase for you."

Tracy heaved a sigh of relief. "Thanks so much. I'd love to have a look at the contents if it's still around." She fervently hoped it was and that someone hadn't donated it to a thrift shop. She realized, though, that was a long shot.

"Even if I locate it, you shouldn't get your hopes up that you'll find a clue inside," Dale cautioned. "The police officers at the time would have gone through the contents in hopes of finding something to help identify the woman or to assist them in locating her family. If they couldn't find anything—which apparently, they didn't—you probably won't either. So don't hold your breath."

"I won't," Tracy promised.

No, she wouldn't hold her breath.

But she would hope for the best.

Chapter Eleven

You're doing quite well, Jana. I'm proud of you." Tracy smiled at her niece, who sat beside her on the piano bench. Tracy had been giving her lessons for the past year and, for the most part, Jana had been diligent with her practice. She'd learned to plunk out "Jingle Bells" and was now working on "Away in a Manger."

Jana grinned. "Thanks, Aunt Tracy."

Tracy slipped her arm around Jana's shoulders and gave her a half hug. "You're looking forward to being an angel in the Christmas pageant, aren't you?"

Jana nodded, and her eyes lit up. "Have you seen my wings? They're all glittery. It's more fun to be an angel than a lamb. I was a lamb last year, remember?"

"I do remember. Your angel wings are beautiful," Tracy said.

She urged Jana to give the song another try, this time without looking at the sheet music.

After Jana finished the song, she glanced up at Tracy and smiled. Tracy smiled back at her. "I think that's enough for the day. You keep practicing."

"Okay," Jana promised.

"I know it's hard to practice at this time of year. There's so much going on at school and at church. And the wedding is coming up too."

Jana's smile slipped.

"I hope you're not feeling too stressed about everything," Tracy went on. "Your mom told me that you had to go to the principal's office because you yelled at Natalie. Do you want to talk about it?"

Jana grimaced and shook her head.

In a slightly more serious tone, Tracy added, "I'm surprised by that behavior. It's not like you, Jana. Natalie must have really made you angry."

With tears filling her eyes, Jana said, "I don't know why I got mad at her. Mom made me apologize, and I did. I..." She left her statement unfinished.

"I hope it won't happen again," Tracy said softly. "I don't want to see you punished. Christmas should be a joyous time remembering the birth of Jesus, singing carols and giving gifts to those we love and to those less fortunate, sharing cookies with neighbors, and all sorts of fun things."

With a quick swipe of her hand across her eyes, Jana sniffed. "I guess I'm just sad about something."

"Can you tell me what it is?" Tracy asked in her most coaxing tone.

"No. You'll get mad at me too, like Mom did."

"Your mom's not mad at you, sweetie. She's more worried than anything else. And a little disappointed in your behavior, of course. But if something is wrong and she doesn't know what it is, she can't fix it." Tracy ducked her head to look Jana in the eyes. "Are you sure you don't want to talk about it while we're here together? No one else is around, and I'm a pretty good listener."

Again, Jana shook her head. "No, Aunt Tracy, not now."

Tracy straightened her shoulders. She'd done her best. There was no use pressing any further. She scooped up the sheet music and placed it in a neat pile on top of the piano. "When you want to talk, you just let me know, okay? I want to help, if I can."

Jana responded with another watery sniff.

Rising from the bench, Tracy leaned over to drop a quick kiss on the top of Jana's head. She was on her way to the kitchen to say goodbye to Amy when Jana shot out a question.

"Aunt Tracy, can I ask you something?"

Tracy turned, smiling. "Sure, sweetie. What is it?"

Jana frowned and firmed her jaw. "When grownups get engaged to be married, do they ever change their minds before the wedding happens? Can they do that? Can they change their minds?" Jana regarded her searchingly.

Tracy hesitated. Where was this question coming from? Was Jana hoping Amy and Miles would change their minds? Or did she fear they would? "Sometimes people do change their minds about getting married. But most of the time they don't. Why do you want to know?"

With a shrug, Jana replied, "Just asking."

Jana's odd question still buzzed around in Tracy's thoughts on Wednesday morning when she returned to the office determined to get her column done and several other tasks she'd shoved to the corner of her desk. Both she and Jeff had gotten up early and taken

Sadie for a walk around the block. Some Christmas lights still glistened in the dawn's early morning light. It was quiet and peaceful and not too cold—just brisk enough to make slight wisps of breath when they spoke to one another.

When Tracy told Jeff what Jana had said, he frowned. "Do you think she's afraid that Amy or Miles will change their minds and not get married? Or do you think she's hoping that they will call the wedding off?"

"I really don't know," Tracy replied.

When she arrived at the office, she hung her coat on the rack near the door and waved at Annette, who was already speaking with someone on the phone. Annette waved back. Tracy's eyes flickered over to Eric's closed door. She couldn't tell if he was in or not. She'd not noticed his car in the parking lot, but then, she hadn't really been looking for it either.

Tracy gave a nod here and there to other employees and chuckled when she read the words on Jake's red sweatshirt. FRIENDS DON'T GIVE FRIENDS FRUITCAKE. Grinning, she made her way to the coffee counter in the break room, her favorite mug in hand. Someone had brought in a platter of apricot kolaches. Tracy happily helped herself to one.

As she left the break room, she checked her stride, coming to an abrupt halt. Eric stood over her desk, rummaging through her inbox. Then he fingered several folded newspapers on the corner of her desk. He muttered something under his breath. Tracy felt a slight trepidation. Was he checking to see what she was working on? Was she going to have to face his sullen attitude again so early in the morning? What was bothering the man?

Mustering every ounce of optimism she could manage under the circumstances, Tracy approached him with a smile. Before she could wish him a good morning, Eric turned to her, eyes questioning. "What's this?" He pointed to the stack of old newspapers.

"Back issues of the *Lewis County Times*," Tracy said. She'd asked Bethany to retrieve the December 1969 issues from the basement.

"I can see that. Why were you reading them?" Eric's frown deepened.

Tracy didn't want to admit that she wanted to read Columbia Burke's follow-up article about the Woman in White—the one Grandma Pearl had urged Columbia to write when she'd joined the newspaper staff. But she didn't want to lie either. "As you can see, they're all December issues. Sometimes I get ideas for my column by reading back issues." This was true enough. She'd done so on numerous occasions.

"What ideas are you pursuing?" Eric inquired.

Tracy could feel herself blushing. His interest made her feel a pang of guilt—irrational guilt. "I haven't had time to go through these yet." And that was certainly true too. She'd just noticed the papers when she'd come in this morning. Tracy resisted the urge to glance over at Annette, who had pushed her chair away from her desk and sat there unabashedly listening to the encounter. Tracy tried to keep her expression calm and neutral.

"Maybe I'll have a quick look too," Eric said, swiping the newspapers from the corner of Tracy's desk. "I'll give them back later." He turned away, returned to his office, and closed the door behind him.

Standing there with a coffee mug in one hand and the pastry in the other, Tracy's mouth hung open as she watched his retreating figure.

Annette sidled up to her and touched her shoulder. "Hey, don't worry about it. Just shrug it off. I don't know what's up with him, but I'm going to find out. I think Eric and I are going to have to have a little talk."

"Please don't do it while I'm here," Tracy pleaded. "He might accuse me of putting you up to it." She took a sip of her cooling coffee.

"If that doesn't work, I'm going to call Doug," Annette declared. "Maybe the stress of the job is getting to Eric."

"Good luck with that," Tracy said.

Although Doug Ledger owned the paper and had a private office here, he'd been spending most of his time in Colorado, close to his cancer doctors.

"Eric's behavior is unprofessional," Annette went on. "Besides that, he's put a real damper on the Christmas spirit around here, and I don't like it." She folded her arms across her chest and frowned at Eric's door.

Sitting down at her desk, Tracy ran her tongue over her lips. She'd have to be more careful about pursuing her investigation. Eric would surely discover Columbia's article in one of those issues if he took the time to go through them. Her interest in the topic seemed to annoy him. She wondered why.

Annette perched on the corner of Tracy's desk. She leaned in close, "I'm going to tell you something, but I don't want you to share it with anyone else."

Tracy wasn't sure she wanted to hear a secret, but she regarded her friend questioningly. Annette wiggled her finger, urging Tracy to move closer before she whispered, "I've heard a rumor that Eric submitted a book manuscript to a big-time New York publisher. He

SECRETS FROM GRANDMA'S ATTIC

received a rejection letter. That could be the reason he's in such a foul mood. Someone said he's been working on that book for years."

Tracy arched an eyebrow. "That might be the explanation, but then again, reporters and journalists are supposed to have thicker skin than most. Besides, don't all writers get rejections at one time or another? Occupational hazard, right?"

Annette rolled her eyes and returned to her own desk. Tracy looked around the office as she took a bite of her kolache. Everyone appeared to be concentrating on their work. She glanced at the clock on the far wall. She didn't want to be late for Amy's bridal shower. Tracy's daughter, Sara, was one of the hostesses. Sara had promised to have her husband bring the rocking chair—complete with a big red bow—that Tracy had bought for Amy's present.

When her cell tweeted, Tracy was surprised to see that it was Dale calling from his personal number. She answered the call expectantly.

"Tracy, I have good news about that suitcase you're trying to find—sort of," Dale told her. She could hear the eagerness in his voice.

"So soon?" A tingling raced along her spine. She swiveled her desk chair around so she could keep an eye on Eric's closed door. If he opened it even one little crack, she intended to cut Dale off. She'd step outside later and call him back. "Wow, that was quick."

"Easy enough, since I had an exact date to start with," Dale went on. "But like I said, it's only sort of good news. I didn't find the suit-case, but I learned that the department held on to it for a year. When they had no inquiries from the woman's relatives or from other law

The Cameo Clue

enforcement agencies, the police chief at the time turned it over to the town council for safekeeping."

Tracy didn't bother to ask for a name. It didn't matter. Whoever the chief handed the suitcase to would have long since passed away. Her best hope was to learn if the present council had a lost and found or a storage room where they kept unclaimed items.

"I'm sorry, Tracy, that's the best I can do," Dale said. "Oh, and there's a black-and white photograph of the deceased in the police files too, if you want to see it. I should warn you though, it was taken at the morgue. You know what I mean? It's not as tasteful as the police sketch."

In her most cheerful voice, Tracy thanked him for his efforts. "That's okay, Dale. I'll pass on looking at the photograph right now. Thanks again. I think I know just the man who can help me from this point on."

"Who might that be?"

"Lincoln Bailey," she replied.

Canton's enthusiastic and friendly head alderman on the city council knew everyone in Canton. He'd been Tracy's best source at the newspaper for many of her stories. As a lawyer, he'd handled Grandma Pearl's estate and had often helped Tracy by providing a necessary clue now and then for the mysteries she'd solved. He also served on the board of trustees for Culver-Stockton College. Lincoln had helped her numerous times in the past—with great results. Tracy felt certain he would be able to do so again.

SECRETS FROM GRANDMA'S ATTIC

August 30, 1944
Oaklawn Retreat
Jacksonville, Illinois

Dear Aunt Violet,

You may be wondering why you haven't heard from me in quite some time. I have been very ill. One day I hemorrhaged when I coughed while sitting quietly in a rocking chair on the screened porch. It felt like something had broken in my chest. I can tell you, I was quite frightened. I was taken immediately to my bed and was forced to stay there for several days. Even had to use a bedpan instead of getting up to use the toilet. I was told not to move or even talk, unless I did so in a whisper.

That has slowed the coughing a little, but I can still feel something in my chest. The doctor ordered another X-ray. This time it showed a cavity in my lung. He and the specialist are considering collapsing my right lung. I don't know what that means. I'm afraid it will hurt dreadfully. Fortunately, the left lung is unaffected.

The specialist's name is Dr. Spooner. He seems so young and friendly, boisterous, even. Not old enough to be a doctor. Do you know what I mean? Doctors should be a little gray-haired and rather like a grandfather. Not Dr. Spooner! He had a notebook and took down my whole life history—really. I had to begin with the day I was born and tell him everything. Where I grew up, about my parents and other relatives like you and Uncle Alfred, and the kind of places we lived and the sort of jobs I worked. He even wanted to know all about Tom. He said he was sorry for my loss. He is a very kind man and optimistic about my eventual recovery, so I am feeling hopeful too. It's a good feeling.

On absolute rest days, I lie flat on one skinny pillow. I'm not allowed to read or write letters. I stare at the ceiling, mostly. I can turn my head from side to side and look at the women in the beds next to mine. That's about it. On moderate rest days, like today, I can have two pillows, and I can read or write if I want. It's awkward trying to eat and drink when ordered to lie flat. And using a bedpan is the worst thing ever. We all make jokes about it, and it's good to hear laughter in the ward.

Despite Dr. Spooner's reassurance, sometimes I feel like I'm not making any progress at all, and it's a bitter disappointment to me, as you can imagine. I thought I was getting better. Isn't that why they sent me here? It's been weeks and weeks. Endless weeks. The visiting minister sat with me a while yesterday, and we talked some. Well, really, he talked, and I listened. He read a few Psalms—ones written when King David was feeling a bit down and depressed. It helped, and I felt better by the time he left. He made me realize how much I miss going to church.

Did I tell you they moved me into a different room? It's nice—only six of us in here. I can see pine trees through the big french doors. A lovely view. The nurses in this wing seem as young as I am. And all are quite pretty. I marvel that they don't worry about catching TB from me and the other patients. One of the patients in the new room with me is only a girl. She's fourteen and as cute as a button. Her name is Mona. She is horrified about being here and told me she started crying the minute they made her take her clothes off and put on the flannel pajamas and robe that we all must wear. She's worried because her parents never come on visitation days. She's been scared since they dropped her off, and I'm doing what I can to make her feel a little better. I told her I don't have visitors either, and that made her feel a little happier, I think.

Of course, there are days when I'm pretty scared myself. I suspect I'm not doing a good job of hiding that from Mona or anyone else. But what if I die here? What if I never get better? What will happen then? Mona thinks the nurses are mean because of all the stuff they do to us, like making us weigh each day and taking our temperature and opening the windows wide even when it's raining and blustery outside.

Mona coughs a lot and cries just as often. She can barely breathe most days, so it's hard for her to even walk to the toilet. And she's so skinny, so frail. I'll bet she doesn't weigh eighty pounds soaking wet! The nurses are doing all they can to fatten her up, but Mona has a stubborn streak. The other day we had pork chops on our dinner tray. Mona cut all the fat off hers and pushed the trimmings to the side. The nurse told her she had to eat the fat with the meat. Mona snapped back that she didn't like the fat and wasn't going eat it no matter what. That night, the nurse never took the tray away. She woke Mona up twice in the middle of the night, ordering her to eat the fat. Mona finally gave in.

A couple of weeks ago, Mona tried to run away. She crawled out of the window and made it to the top of the hill, where she saw some construction workers. One of them asked her what she was doing running around in her pajamas like that. She explained that she ran away from the sanatorium because of how mean they treated her. One of the men brought her right back. Apparently, she was a mess. One braid had come loose, and her pajamas and robe were dirt streaked, her socks were filthy, and one slipper was missing. She had a skinned knee too. I didn't see all this, because I was out on the porch getting my daily dose of sunshine and fresh air.

The doctor locked Mona in a solitary room for one whole week. When she was allowed to come back to our room, she cried telling me all about it. Her thin shoulders shook. I felt so sad for her. I could feel a lump in my throat, but I refused to cry. I'm afraid once I get started, I won't be able to stop. I'm always feeling sorry for myself as it is, but I keep remembering what Jilly said about keeping my chin up. Besides, crying will make me cough, and coughing hurts my chest.

Mona is more compliant now. Still, Nurse Booth came in with the book of rules and read them aloud to us. I think she did this mainly for Mona's benefit. The rules say that any patient who cannot adapt herself to the necessary restrictions must inform the medical superintendent so that arrangements for the patient's discharge can be made. The rules go on to warn patients that we must not disregard the rules. Doing so can hinder the staff and make matters more difficult for our fellow patients.

Of course, it is completely forbidden to consume any alcoholic beverages on the premises, and there's to be no communication between patients of the opposite sex. Men are in one wing, and women are in another. Nurse Booth even cautioned us against saying "Good morning" when we pass a man on the grounds. As I'm not allowed to wander about, that will not be too difficult to keep in mind, although it seems unnecessarily rude to ignore them, don't you think?

As you can imagine, I have a lot of time to think about things. I've become aware that many people die here. I guess I didn't realize that at first. People come here to get cured, right? But one morning, we woke up and there was an empty bed across the room. The nurse explained that the woman had died in the night. Some days I feel a heavy burden of terror and tedium. Just yesterday, I'd spent most of the day on the porch. When I returned to my room, a bed was being stripped and remade for the next patient. A young woman named Elspeth had passed away during our afternoon nap-time. She was here, and now she's gone—forever.

Did I tell you there's a cemetery on the grounds? One of the nurses told me that because of the fear and stigma associated with this disease, some of the patients' families don't claim the bodies of their relatives for burial. Others never even have visits from their family members who live right in town.

I had a letter from Jilly this past week. She says she'll come see me if she can get some time off. It's about two hours by bus, she says. I'm so excited about her coming. She's always been a breath of fresh air. She's going to bring me some fudge too. I'm looking forward to that. Her upcoming visit makes me wonder, would you and Uncle Alfred come visit me sometime soon? Would you be willing? Could you bring Dory too? A visit would cheer me up. I can't tell you how much.

Your hopeful niece,

Trula

Chapter Twelve

Blushing with pleasure, Amy said, "Thank you, everyone. You've made me feel very special." She looked around at the teachers congregated in the school library where the bridal shower had taken place. She winked at Tracy.

Tracy smiled. It had been a lovely shower complete with blue and white streamers and paper snowflakes fluttering from the library ceiling. The lemon-filled coconut cupcakes had been as pretty as they were delicious. Instead of punch, Sara and the other hostesses had set up a hot chocolate bar complete with all sorts of fancy stir-ins—marshmallows, tinted whipped cream, and an assortment of sprinkles and syrups.

Amy received many practical gifts and several gift cards. As both she and Miles had been homeowners for quite some time, they didn't need many of the typical items that most newlyweds needed. And of course, Amy had loved the rocking chair.

"Oh Tracy, you shouldn't have," she declared when she saw it beside the gift table. Amy gave her a hearty hug.

"I knew you'd love it," Tracy said with a light laugh, hugging her back. "It isn't every day my only sister gets married. I wanted to give you something special." She hoped that her sister would be as blessed in her marriage as she and Jeff had been for so many years.

"I do love it, and I know just where I'm going to put it when we move into Miles's house."

Before leaving, Tracy snapped some photos of the school librarian standing in front of the display of Christmas read-aloud books that were on display for students and their families. Tracy had called her the previous week, asking if she would make a few recommendations for her to print in the newspaper. The librarian, a lanky young woman with pink-tinted hair, had been delighted to do so.

Tracy had even taken a few photos of Amy opening presents and the shower hostesses standing in front of the hot chocolate bar. If Eric wanted more "local color" articles, she could write up a story about the popular Canton school teacher and her holiday bridal shower. It would be a good piece for the Lifestyle section of the paper.

Tracy stepped outside, shivering inside her warm jacket. The sky had taken on a steely gray color. It had grown colder, and the wind had picked up, freezing her cheeks and nose. She hurried to her vehicle. It just might snow tonight, although there hadn't been snow in the morning's forecast.

As soon as she left the school grounds, Tracy headed to Lincoln Bailey's office, which was located on the second floor above Pop Rocks Vintage. She parked near the curb and retrieved the scrapbook. Recognizing Melody Bailey's vehicle in the next parking space, Tracy bounded up the steps, expecting to see Lincoln's wife as well.

Melody greeted her with a bright smile. The attractive woman looked stunning in a red blazer that complemented her graying hair nicely. Melody was an experienced accountant and had served on the church's finance committee for many years.

SECRETS FROM GRANDMA'S ATTIC

"Hi, Melody. Are you pinch-hitting as secretary today?" Tracy asked, noting that Melody stood behind the secretary's desk, looking through one of the drawers. A huge poinsettia had been placed on one corner of the desk. Sometimes, Erica, the Baileys' daughter, worked in the office between semesters, but Tracy guessed she was still away at college in upstate New York and had not returned home yet for the Christmas break.

"Yes, poor Maria is out with the flu." She glanced down at an open date book in the center of the desk. "You don't have an appointment with Lincoln, do you? I don't see your name anywhere."

"No, I don't. If Lincoln is too busy to see me, I can make an appointment or give him a call later. I just have a quick question or two. Nothing that can't wait."

Tracy meant what she said. The unidentified woman buried in the cemetery had remained nameless for nearly eighty years. A few more days—even a few more weeks or months—wouldn't really matter. She only hoped she could eventually solve the mystery, that it would not prove to be a lost cause.

Melody gave her a nod before knocking lightly on the closed door of her husband's private office. She opened it just a little and poked her head inside. Tracy heard her say, "Tracy Doyle is here, if you have a minute."

Tracy couldn't hear his response, but in a matter of seconds, Lincoln made an appearance, opening the door wide and striding forward, ready to shake her hand. "Tracy Doyle, one of my favorite constituents and a favorite client," he said jovially in his deep rumble of a voice.

Tracy grinned. "I'll bet you say that to all your visitors."

The Cameo Clue

"In what capacity are you here today?"

"Both, I think," Tracy said. Lincoln gave her a quizzical glance. As Melody prepared to leave them alone, Tracy turned and said, "It's not a private matter, Melody. Please stay. You may be able to help me too."

Turning again to Lincoln, Tracy said, "I understand the city council took possession of a suitcase almost eighty years ago that belonged to a mysterious stranger—a very ill woman—who arrived in Canton by bus, collapsed on the sidewalk, and died shortly afterwards."

Lincoln frowned, but Melody nodded eagerly. "You're talking about the Woman in White!"

Tracy could feel her eyes widen. "I am. Do you know anything about her?"

"Indeed I do. Your husband isn't the only history buff in town."

"I'm lost," Lincoln admitted. "Come in, both of you. Sit down and tell me what you're talking about."

"You might want to look at this first," Tracy said, handing him the scrapbook. "My grandmother was so intrigued by the story that she kept a variety of newspaper clippings regarding the woman's death and burial."

As Lincoln flipped through the scrapbook, Melody peered over his shoulder. Tracy sat in a chair across from the lawyer's impressive desk—the same chair she'd sat in many times before when Lincoln helped settle Grandma Pearl's estate.

"Grandma Pearl even has the cameo brooch the woman is wearing in the sketch. I have that at home. Apparently, my grandmother thought it might come in handy in helping to identify the woman. A family heirloom that a relative might recognize."

SECRETS FROM GRANDMA'S ATTIC

Melody shook her head, saying, "As far as I know, no one has ever stepped forward to ID the woman or the brooch."

Lincoln looked at his wife with admiring surprise. "Mel, how do you know so much about this?"

Melody chuckled. "I've been on the church finance committee a long time. One of the things I volunteered to do some years ago was to computerize the old financial records. It just so happens that the records go back years and years—decades even. The church paid for the casket for that young woman. The minister at the time did the service for free, and various community members donated to a benevolent fund for the headstone."

"I had no idea," Lincoln said.

"Anyway, the incident intrigued me," Melody went on. "I began looking into it. Tawny Hagstrom helped. What's most intriguing is the bouquet of white roses left on the grave each December up until a few years ago. No one ever found out who was responsible for the kind remembrance." Turning to Tracy, she said, "Don't you think it's rather romantic, that someone secretly loved her so much?"

"I'm not sure it's a romantic gesture," Tracy replied somewhat hesitantly. "I think red roses are a sign of romantic love, right? And if her lover or fiancé or husband loved her so much, why didn't he step forward?"

Melody shrugged. "I've always wondered about that."

"At this late stage in the game, I doubt we'll ever know," Lincoln said.

Melody pointed to the police sketch. "I wish they'd taken a photograph though. A sketch doesn't show her pallor or other signs of her illness. It was reported that she was quite ill with tuberculosis."

The Cameo Clue

"Sergeant Dale Leewright told me today there is a photo, but it was taken at the morgue after she died," Tracy said.

"Too bad," Lincoln said, shaking his head and regarding the sketch thoughtfully. "Such a shame. She was obviously young."

"I need to do some research on that disease," Tracy said. "I really know very little about it."

"I had an aunt who suffered with TB," Melody said. "She couldn't go to a sanatorium. They didn't accept African Americans at the time."

"What happened to her?" Tracy asked.

"They sent her away to live with a cousin in Arizona. TB is very infectious. All that heavy coughing spreads germs. Back in the early forties there was little one could do for TB patients. Fresh air, good hygiene, decent food. Those seemed to be the only remedies. But it could take a year or two to get well. Many people died from it until right after World War II when streptomycin and other antibiotics were discovered. Then the death rate dropped by more than half."

Tracy asked, "Did your aunt survive?"

Melody shook her head. "Sadly, no. She'd been having chest pains and shortness of breath for such a long time. She didn't go to a doctor until long after she'd started coughing up blood. By then it was too late for the rest cure. The disease was too far gone."

After listening to Melody's account, Tracy had an idea. "I wonder if Grandma Pearl thought to contact TB asylums or sanatoriums." She looked from Melody to Lincoln.

"I couldn't say," Lincoln said. "Your grandmother never spoke of this to me." He closed the scrapbook and handed it back to Tracy. "Now what's this about a missing suitcase?"

SECRETS FROM GRANDMA'S ATTIC

Tracy told him what Dale had told her. "Is it possible that the suitcase is stashed in a storage room or some unused office? If so, and if you can find it, I'd like to go through it and look for clues."

Lincoln gave her a crooked smile. "You're a lot like your grandmother, Tracy—a real optimist. Why do you think after all this time you could find a clue when others haven't?"

Melody smiled also. "The police surely looked it over, and I imagine the doctor and the minister did too. Maybe even your grandmother."

Tracy sighed. "Yes, that's what Dale told me. But he wished me luck nonetheless."

Lincoln rolled his chair away from the desk. He leaned back, lacing his fingers across his stomach. "I don't know how much good it will do, but I'll have someone look around for it. For all we know, it was given away to a thrift shop or to a church that collects clothing for the needy."

Tracy sighed. That seemed like the logical thing to do, particularly when no one ever stepped forward to identify the woman and claim her meager belongings. She could feel her shoulders slump.

"Hey, don't give up yet," Lincoln encouraged her. "I'll do what I can to locate that suitcase, if it's still around."

Melody gave her husband an approving pat on the shoulder. Then with a smile for Tracy, she said, "In the meantime, maybe you can pursue another angle."

"Like what?"

"The local flower shop. Fancy Floral. It's been in the same location for a long time. Different owners off and on over the years."

The Cameo Clue

"Yes, I've been meaning to get around to that," Tracy said. "There just aren't enough hours in the day."

"The original building was renovated some years ago," Lincoln said. "Part of Canton's desire to keep downtown's historic businesses in good shape for the tourist trade. Who knows? Maybe florists keep good records like the church." Then he added, "But don't get your hopes up, Tracy."

"Look, someone bought those flowers each December to place on the grave." Apparently Melody refused to have the suggestion dismissed so lightly. "They did it for decades."

Tracy felt a spark of determination. She'd made up her mind to check out the flower shop, and she needed to do it, sooner rather than later. "You're right. And several people would have had to be in on the secret. It was passed from one generation to the next. No one person could live long enough to keep the tradition alive."

"It's possible that someone purchased the flowers right here in Canton," Melody pointed out.

"Or maybe they went out of town to make the purchase so they wouldn't be recognized," Lincoln proposed. "The identity of the deceased woman isn't the only mystery here."

Would the flowers have been a special order? Perhaps Elaine McLaren, the woman Annette recommended she speak with, would know. Tracy rose with a new eagerness to finally pursue this lead. "Thanks for your help. I need to get going on this."

Melody nodded her approval. "You may learn who purchased the flowers, but that individual may not have known the identity of the deceased woman. The gesture may have simply been a sentimental one. The doctor, for instance, may have wished to remember the poor young woman he couldn't save."

"That's a possibility I'd not considered," Tracy said. "But you're right, Christmas is a sentimental time of year. Still, it doesn't explain why the doctor would have kept placing flowers on the grave for so many years. And who took up the tradition when the doctor passed away?"

"Another mystery," Melody said, lifting her hands in a who-knows gesture.

Tracy bit her lip and glanced at the clock on the wall. It was getting late. She wanted to stop by the office to download the photos she'd taken that day before going home. "Again, thanks for all your help. I realize now that this is more complicated than I originally thought. No wonder Grandma Pearl quit pursuing it."

Lincoln rose too. "I'm sure Pearl did her best. She may have decided there was nothing more she could do for the Woman in White but to let her rest in peace."

Rest in peace? Tracy considered the proverbial statement for a moment. What about the family who never knew what had happened to her—their long-lost daughter or sister, mother or friend? What about them? Did they—could they—rest in peace?

Chapter Thirteen

hursday morning, Tracy pulled into the parking lot at the newspaper office just as Annette climbed out of her own vehicle. Bundled up in a dark gray knee-length coat with a red-and-gray plaid scarf, Annette raised a hand in greeting and then waited for Tracy to catch up with her on the sidewalk.

"It's true. Eric received a rejection letter from Simon & Schuster," Annette whispered in a conspiratorial tone. "I saw the letter on the corner of his desk yesterday after he left."

"You were in his office?" Tracy arched an eyebrow. "You read the letter?"

Annette rolled her eyes. "I had some letters from readers for him, and I placed them on his desk. The rejection letter was right there—plain as day—open for anyone to see. I couldn't help but read it. Don't say you wouldn't have done the same. Journalists are all snoops. We can't help ourselves."

Tracy couldn't deny that. Her curiosity meter was always soaring to the top of the charts. "So he really is writing a book. Is it a novel? A biography? Could you tell from the letter?"

Shaking her head, Annette scrunched the scarf up closer around her ears. Tracy tugged at her own. The breeze was brisk, more uncomfortable than invigorating. "I have no idea. Let's get inside. It's cold out here."

They took several long strides before darting into the office building. Tracy glanced over at Eric's office. The door was closed. The light wasn't on. Apparently, he hadn't come in yet, which was unusual for the editor-in-chief, who often worked long hours and appeared to live at the office.

"Such a letter would certainly explain his grumpy mood," Tracy murmured as they removed their coats and hung them on the rack near the door. "It's never any fun receiving a rejection, but it must be even more disappointing at Christmas."

"No doubt he was hoping Santa Claus would bring him a nice juicy book contract, complete with a generous advance," Annette quipped. "Still, his disappointment is no excuse for treating the staff the way he has been." She glanced over her shoulder to make sure no one else was listening. "It's not our fault his manuscript was rejected. As I said before, I'm thinking of having a word with him."

"Good luck," Tracy said.

At her desk, she rummaged through the contents of her inbox. Nothing appeared urgent or time sensitive. She tackled a few tasks, purged some emails, and then decided to visit Fancy Floral. Ever since Annette had suggested it as a place where she might dig up a clue, Tracy had been eager to see what she could discover there. Who had purchased the white rose bouquet each year? And why? Her active imagination could conjure several tantalizing theories.

After scribbling a few lines on a sticky note, she made her way to Edmund Grant's desk. The Lifestyle editor was already hard at work. She could see him laying out pages on his computer for the next day's online edition. He looked up and smiled at her approach.

"Hi Edmund. I don't know if you're interested in running a piece about Amy Allen's bridal shower, but I've written down the pertinent facts and emailed them to you along with some photos. Amy's a first-grade teacher at the elementary school. Her colleagues got together yesterday to host a shower for her. I've double-checked the spelling of the hostesses' names too."

"Thanks, Tracy. I don't think I'll have room for it in next week's print edition, but maybe the one after that." He took the paper she handed him.

"Actually, she's getting married next month. And," she added with a half-smile, "in full disclosure, I should tell you that Amy is my little sister."

Edmund chuckled. "That explains why you attended the shower then, doesn't it? I don't generally get invited to events like that. Not that I mind very much. Baby and bridal showers aren't my thing." His phone rang. "Have to take this," he said, dismissing her with a nod.

Tracy gave him a thumbs-up and returned to her desk. She gave her calendar a glance and decided she'd done enough for the day. Besides, she wanted to scoot out before Eric showed up. She didn't relish being the object of his wrath again today if she could help it.

"I'm outta here," she called to Annette. Her friend was on the phone but raised a hand in acknowledgment of Tracy's departure.

After retrieving her coat from the rack, Tracy made her way out the door. She sincerely hoped Eric wasn't pulling into the parking lot about now. He might ask her where she was off to, and she didn't want to tell him that she intended to visit the floral shop, hoping to discover the identity of the person who put the roses on the Woman in White's grave. Grandma Pearl had always been adamant about not lying. "Tell the truth and shame the devil," she'd often said. It was good advice.

Fancy Floral was located near Buttermilk Bakeshop. Noting this, Tracy made up her mind to treat herself to hot tea and a chocolate chip scone when her interview was over. Flinging her purse strap over her shoulder, she retrieved the scrapbook from the front seat of her car. She then strode through the door of the floral shop. A little bell jingled her arrival. The festive window display sported artificial snow and a gingerbread village flanked by potted poinsettias and freesia. She also noted the pleasant aromas mingled in the store—the scent of roses, the spicy scent of carnations, and something that smelled citrusy.

"Good morning, may I help you?" The young salesclerk greeted her with a cheery smile. She was quite tall and wore a sprig of fake holly tucked inside her cornrows.

"I hope so," Tracy replied with a smile of her own. "I'd like to have a word with the owner, if I could. That would be Gwen Montgomery, right?" Tracy had looked that up on the store's website.

The clerk's smile faltered a little. Just a little. Her dark eyes flickered to the scrapbook Tracy had under one arm. "Yes, Gwen is in her office. May I give her your name?"

"I'm Tracy Doyle," she replied with a sunny smile. Tracy didn't want to put the salesclerk or the owner of the shop on their guard. This was a friendly visit—nothing to be concerned about.

The young woman's eyes widened. She came from around the counter to the office door, walking past a stunning display of Christmas cactus. She knocked and then poked her head inside.

The Cameo Clue

"There's a Tracy Doyle here to see you." After a moment she turned and said, "Gwen will see you now."

"Thanks so much," Tracy said, and entered the office. A middle-aged woman sat behind a tidy, well-organized desk dotted with a colorful array of glass paperweights. She had short-cropped strawberry blond hair and appealing dimples in both cheeks. Gwen rose as Tracy approached the desk, and invited her to have a seat.

"I'm intrigued, Tracy Doyle. I've seen your articles in the *Lewis County Times*. Are you here to do a story about my shop?" Her tone was hopeful.

Tracy sat down and dropped her purse beside the chair. Balancing the scrapbook on her lap, she said, "I'm sorry, no, I'm not here to do a story. I guess you could say I'm on a personal quest."

Gwen leaned forward, her elbows propped on the desk, her fingers laced together. "Now I really am intrigued. A little disappointed too, I'll admit. I would love to have some photos of the store in the paper so customers can see what we have to offer. I purchased an ad a week or so ago, but it's not the same as color photos. But I'm still intrigued by your quest."

With a wide smile, Tracy declared, "I can arrange to have photos taken for the newspaper. Easy peasy. And I'd be happy to do so. Your store is beautiful. And it smells so good too." Eric was always looking for "local color," as he called it, to fill the paper. Hadn't she just provided a photo of the nativity set on the lawn of the Baptist church and the impressive poinsettia tree in the foyer of Faith Church?

"I'll send a text to our staff photographer and ask him to stop by. What time is convenient for you?" Tracy reached into her coat pocket for her cell phone.

SECRETS FROM GRANDMA'S ATTIC

Beaming, Gwen sat up a little straighter. "Anytime that works for you, anytime at all."

Tracy tapped out a text to Nick, the staff photographer, giving him the details. That done, she turned with another smile to Gwen. "You should hear from him soon. We can put an article in the next time we have room for a local story. Now I'm wondering if you can help me."

"I'll certainly try." The woman appeared eager to cooperate.

Tracy passed her the scrapbook. "I found this in my grandmother's attic. It's all about an unidentified woman who died here in Canton back in December of 1944. For many years, someone anonymously placed a bouquet of white roses on her grave every December. I don't suppose you know anything about the incident—it happened so long ago—but I'm wondering if the bouquets came from this shop. Do you have records from the previous owners?"

Gwen flipped through the scrapbook, glancing at some pages and studying others more closely. She paused at the page with the police sketch. "The Woman in White. Yes, I know a little about the flowers for her grave."

Tracy's heart flipped over. "Really? What do you know, exactly?"

"I know that the bouquets were ordered from this shop for decades. At least, that's what the previous owner told me. I bought the store about five years ago, and no one has placed an order for a bouquet of white roses for the grave since then. Of course, that doesn't mean they didn't buy flowers of a different sort from us and then take them to the cemetery." She shrugged. "You should talk to Elaine McLaren."

Tracy's ears perked up. There was that name again.

"She worked for the previous two owners," Gwen went on. "I was told that each December someone ordered a bouquet. That person paid in cash. Sometimes the flowers were to be delivered to the cemetery and placed on the grave. At other times, Elaine personally delivered the bouquet to the person who ordered it. As I said, there hasn't been an order like that since I took over ownership."

"Did Elaine ever mention who the customer was?" Tracy probed.

Gwen shook her head. "You need to speak with Elaine. The previous owner advised me to place a larger than usual order for white roses from our supplier each December. I did that for the first couple of years after I took over, but I don't do so any longer, and so far no one has asked me to deliver roses to the grave." She shook her head sadly. "Frankly, I'm a little disappointed. It would be fun to be part of Canton's legendary mystery."

Biting the inside of her cheek, Tracy silently digested this information. How was it possible for someone to keep a secret for such a long time? "My husband and I went to visit the cemetery the other day. There were no flowers on her grave."

"Like I said, if you want the inside scoop on all this, you really need to speak with Elaine McLaren. She lives in a nursing home now, but she worked here for years. I've called her a number of times asking for advice about where to order specialty items that we don't normally carry. She's a font of floral information."

Tracy became aware of the slight uptick of her pulse. Annette had made the same suggestion—speak with Elaine. It was definitely time she did so.

"There isn't anything she doesn't know about this business," Gwen went on. "I think if she'd had the money she might have bought the store herself years ago. She's the one who would know all about the rose bouquets."

Tracy tilted her head. "But you did ask her about them, right?"

Gwen laughed. She closed the scrapbook and handed it to Tracy. "Sure I did. Elaine knows all but won't tell all. So don't get your hopes up. I've tried off and on over the years to pry the secret from her, but she keeps it like a sacred trust." She sat back in her chair, crossing her arms over her chest. "But time passes, things change. Like I said, no one has placed a special order of white roses for the woman's grave since I've owned the store. That doesn't mean the secret benefactor isn't buying flowers from the supermarket or from the florist in Monticello. I don't know."

Gwen rose, announcing the end of the interview. "You need to speak with Elaine."

Chapter Fourteen

"Is that vintage pinball machine still for sale?" Tracy entered her cousin's antique store, the bell tinkling a welcome behind her. She carried a sack of gingerbread scones from Buttermilk Bakeshop.

"And hello to you too," Robin greeted her. After placing a rag doll on a miniature chair, she turned from the attractive holiday window display of other vintage toys that included several old-fashioned spinning tops, a sprightly rocking horse, and a Victorian dollhouse.

Millie Ettlinger, who was waiting on a customer at the counter, nodded and smiled as Tracy entered.

Tracy glanced around the store. It was such an inviting place to shop with a wide variety of merchandise—some antique and some vintage. Robin had once explained the difference to her, but Tracy had forgotten. The shelves were well-stocked but not overcrowded. There were plenty of items to admire, even if one wasn't an antique collector. It was truly an Aladdin's treasure cave. The place sparkled with an assortment of colored glass and beaded handbags from the 1950s. An Amish quilt hung on one wall. Old-fashioned gilt-framed mirrors hung on another. Fairy lights and some artificial evergreen garlands dangled overhead. Art deco lamps glowed dimly, reflecting their light on the polished floors and beamed ceiling.

SECRETS FROM GRANDMA'S ATTIC

Although Robin frequently resupplied her stock, the black-velvet display with their grandmother's pearl necklace in the front window was the one thing that remained the same. Robin had poured her whole heart into making the small business a success, and Grandma Pearl had been tickled pink when Robin named the store Pearls of Wisdom in her honor.

"Yes, the pinball machine is still for sale," Robin told her. Placing her hands on her hips, she tipped her head in the direction of the item Matt had been longing for.

"I'm glad. I want to buy it." Tracy presented her with the bag of scones.

Robin accepted it with a lopsided grin. "What's this? A bribe?" Her face lit up when she peered inside. "Scones. Yummy, and timely too. I just put on a pot of coffee. Follow me."

"There's one for you too, Millie," Tracy said as she passed the counter.

Millie looked up from the cash register to give her another smile.

Tracy stepped into the back room where the aroma of coffee mingled with the faint scent of a citrusy cleaner. She'd bought half a dozen scones for Robin and her employees to enjoy. As she followed Robin, Tracy was glad she'd brought enough. Poppy Maldonado was there, sitting at the worktable, armed with a cotton swab and surrounded by an assortment of figurines. The tall, middle-aged woman sported a candy-cane-striped headband in her dark blond hair. She smiled when she saw Tracy. "Merry Christmas," she said.

"Merry Christmas to you too," Tracy replied. She liked Poppy, who kept the store clean and sparkling—no small job considering the number of surfaces that had to be dusted and polished.

128

The Cameo Clue

Robin placed the scones on the small counter near the coffee-pot. "Want some coffee, Tracy?"

"No, thanks. I've had my limit for the day," Tracy assured her. She'd arrived at the age when too much caffeine kept her awake at night. Sometimes it even gave her heartburn. What was that saying Aunt Ruth often used? Old age isn't for sissies, or something like that. Tracy suspected that might be all too true.

"Poppy, help yourself to a scone," Robin called out as she poured herself a cup of coffee.

Tracy strolled over to the worktable. "What are you working on?"

Poppy held up a porcelain figurine of a dancing woman in a long dress with a ruffled petticoat. "I'm trying to get the dust out of the creases in her skirt," she said. The table was littered with cotton swabs, dustcloths, rubbing alcohol, and other stuff Tracy couldn't put a name to.

"Is it valuable?" asked.

Robin joined them, coffee in one hand and a scone in the other. "Not really. This kind of figurine was mass produced a hundred years ago, and they're regaining in popularity. If I price them reasonably, they'll sell like hotcakes, but not with all the dust and grime in the creases. Poppy has kindly agreed to clean them before I display them on the store shelves."

"Hey, why not? It's Christmastime, and I can always use the extra money," Poppy said.

"The scones are gingerbread," Tracy said. "I brought plenty."

"Thanks, Tracy. I want to finish this lady first." Poppy held up the figurine for inspection. It already looked much better than the ones that had not yet been cleaned.

Robin led the way toward a small table with two chairs in the tiny kitchenette. She gestured for Tracy to have a seat. "I bought the figurines for a song at an estate sale over in Quincy. Like I said, they'll sell quickly once Poppy works her magic." She settled down in one of the chairs. "So, you want to buy the pinball machine?" Robin arched an eyebrow.

"Yes, for Matt for Christmas," Tracy explained. "Amy says he's dying to have it. I thought I'd give it to all four kids—Matt, Jana, Natalie, and Colton. One big gift instead of four individual ones. What do you think?"

"I think it's a good idea." Robin took another bite of her scone. When she'd finished chewing, she added, "In fact, it's such a good idea that I'm going to make you a deal you can't refuse. I'll sell it to you at half price if you'll put my name, Terry's, and Kai's on the gift tag too. I've been trying to figure out what to give the kids for Christmas. This will do. What do you think?"

Tracy beamed. "It's a deal."

"I'll put a sold sign on the machine and have Lash deliver it whenever you're ready," Robin added.

Lash O'Toole was another of Robin's employees. A retired carpenter, he now worked part-time restoring pieces of old furniture that Robin picked up here and there. He was a little rough around the edges, but Tracy liked him nonetheless. Lash was a hard worker and often went the extra mile for Robin and her customers.

"Where do you want it delivered, by the way?" Robin asked. "Your place? Amy's?"

Tracy sighed. "Let me think about that. I'm not sure where it should go. If I have it delivered to Amy's, she'll have to haul it out

The Cameo Clue

again when she and the kids move in with Miles next month. I'll have the same problem if Lash brings it to my place for Christmas Day. It could get damaged from all the moving around."

"Okay, you think about." Robin took another sip of coffee. "What have you been doing today besides Christmas shopping for the kids?"

Tracy leaned back against the chair. "I'm trying to solve another mystery. Amy and I found something rather intriguing in Grandma Pearl's attic this past weekend."

"Don't you always?" Robin cocked an eyebrow. "What is it this time? Something I can eventually sell in the store?"

"Not hardly. It's a scrapbook with old newspaper articles about an unidentified young woman who died here in Canton back in December of 1944. No one ever identified her. She's buried at the cemetery on the edge of town with a headstone that simply reads 'The Woman in White,' along with the date of her death. Jeff and I went out there to see it the other day."

Tracy filled her cousin in on the scrapbook's contents and her conversation with Gwen.

Robin leaned in closer after wiping crumbs from her fingers with a paper napkin. "Tracy, you're right. This is intriguing."

"She arrived with a suitcase," Tracy went on, "and I'm hoping Lincoln Bailey can help me track that down."

"Good luck with that," Robin said. After Tracy explained about the roses, Robin added, "Maybe it was Grandma Pearl who put the bouquet there, since she took such an interest in the poor woman."

Tracy sat up straighter. "Wow, I hadn't even thought of that! Maybe she did. But why would she do it secretly and not let anyone know?"

Robin shrugged.

"Jeff and I talked about it some and wondered if maybe the woman had been having an affair and that she arrived in Canton to meet her lover. Perhaps he was a married man reluctant to step forward to identify her. Filled with remorse, he placed the roses on her grave and did so each year—at least until five years ago. That's when the roses stopped appearing."

Robin frowned. "If that's the case, he sure had a lot of remorse," she said. "And he must have lived to a ripe old age."

"I know," Tracy said. "And that's another mystery. Presumably, the person who started the tradition was an adult. After seventy-plus years, would they have still been able to clandestinely put flowers on the grave?" She grinned. "I mean, Grandma Pearl was spry, but I don't think even she could have snuck to the graveyard by herself when she was ninety-seven."

"This story gets more and more intriguing," Robin said, her eyes sparkling with interest. "It's like an onion. You peel away one layer, and there's another mystery underneath."

Tracy nodded. Her cousin's description was a good one. "And before you ask, yes, I wanted to know if the florist kept records from the past, hoping she'd be able to give me the customer's name. Apparently, the transactions were all made in cash. Gwen did hint that one past employee might be able to provide a clue to the customer's identity if I can get her to tell me. Annette also suggested I talk to her."

"Really? Who?"

"A woman named Elaine McLaren," Tracy said. "She lives at Brookdale. She's confined to a wheelchair but is apparently still sharp as a tack."

Poppy joined them, hovering at Tracy's elbow. Her cheeks appeared flushed, her expression puzzled. When Robin offered her the bag of gingerbread scones, Poppy ignored the gesture. Fixing Tracy with an intent stare, she said, "I couldn't help overhearing your conversation, and I don't mean to be nosy or anything, but did I hear you mention the name Elaine McLaren?"

Tracy nodded and sat up a little straighter. "Do you know her? She worked at Fancy Floral for many years, but she's retired now and living in a nursing home—or so I've been told."

The flush on Poppy's cheeks deepened, and so did her puzzled frown. "I do know her. I know her quite well. Elaine McLaren is my grandmother."

Chapter Fifteen

Tracy's mouth dropped open. Could it really be this easy? "Your grandmother?"

Poppy nodded. "Why do you want to meet her? Are you investigating a case or something? Is she involved in some way?"

Tracy hastened to assure her that Elaine McLaren had done nothing wrong as far as she knew. She gave Poppy a brief summary of the Woman in White conundrum and the bouquet left on the grave each year around Christmastime. "That's why I'd like to speak with her. To find out who ordered the bouquet."

"Nana would know, I'm sure," Poppy said, brightening. "She worked in that floral shop for years. Practically ran the place. I often spent time there doing my homework when I was kid. In fact, I went with her once to place the bouquet on the grave. White roses tied up with a red velvet ribbon."

Robin and Tracy exchanged eager glances. "You did?" Tracy could hear the excitement in her own voice. Now they were getting somewhere.

Poppy raised a finger. "But I should mention Nana was doing it as a favor for a customer. She didn't purchase the flowers herself. It wasn't uncommon for the staff to deliver flowers and wreaths to the cemetery, especially on Memorial Day and Mother's Day or other special occasions."

The Cameo Clue

Tracy smiled. "Poppy, would it be okay if I went to talk to your grandmother?" she asked. "I don't want to wear her out with probing questions or anything. But I do want to meet her and see if she can shed any light on the bouquet purchases. I bought a poinsettia for her while I was at Fancy Floral that I'd like to take her."

With a beaming smile, Poppy said, "How nice! Nana loves flowers—as you may have guessed. If Robin doesn't mind, I'd like to go with you. Can we go now? Nana loves visitors too. She's always been a people person, you know? That's why she was a good employee at the shop. I'll bet there isn't a soul at Brookdale she doesn't know on a first-name basis. She probably knows the names of their kids and grandkids too. I'm sure she'd love to meet you. She reads your column in the newspaper every week, you know."

Robin invited herself along, and before anyone could say "jingle all the way," the three of them were headed to the nursing home in Tracy's vehicle. As Tracy walked through the front doors, she felt quivery with excitement. She was going to meet someone intimately involved with the Woman in White mystery.

The first thing she noticed was the towering Christmas tree decorated with silver lights and silver and blue ornaments. The front desk was festooned with garlands. Some of the employees and even a few of the residents wore Santa hats, which contributed to the festive atmosphere. Christmas carols played in the background, and glittering paper snowflakes hung from the ceiling. A few were mounted on the walls here and there. She wondered if the decorating had been done for the residents' benefit, or to make guests—especially children—feel welcome during the holidays and more inclined to visit. Perhaps a little of both.

135

SECRETS FROM GRANDMA'S ATTIC

Poppy led the way down the hall to her grandmother's room. Tracy and Robin had to step lively to keep up with her long-legged stride. Holding the poinsettia plant in both hands, Tracy again expressed her hope that she wasn't being intrusive.

"Nana loves having visitors, like I told you," Poppy reassured her. "There are many people who don't like nursing homes. They think they're depressing and don't feel comfortable coming here. But everyone in Nana's wing is alert and friendly and eager to talk to visitors." Then she hesitated midstride. "You do know that my grandmother is in a wheelchair, right?"

"Someone mentioned it," Tracy replied.

"Nana was involved in a car accident some years ago, which was followed by a less than successful hip surgery. She can't really get around much without the chair. Otherwise, though, she's as fit as a fiddle for her age. And she'll love the poinsettia. She loves all kinds of plants."

"She must have been a great employee at Fancy Floral," Robin said.

Poppy nodded. "If Nana's not in her room, she'll be down the hall in the library. She has a private room, so you can visit as long as you like. Did you want me to leave after I introduce you, so you can have some privacy?"

"No, not at all," Tracy said. "I'm sure she'll feel much more comfortable answering my questions if you're present."

Poppy tapped lightly on a door that was already slightly open. "Nana, I've brought a visitor to see you." She pushed the door open wider, stepping aside so Tracy and Robin could inch past her into the room.

The Cameo Clue

Elaine McLaren sat at a card table working on a jigsaw puzzle. She looked up, a hopeful expression on her round, cheerful face. She had snow-white hair and bright blue eyes. Her royal-blue sweatshirt boasted a Peter Pan collar and a snowman in the middle. Miniature candy cane earrings dangled from her ears. "Poppy, honey!" Then her curious gaze slid over in Tracy and Robin's direction. "And who did you bring with you?"

"Nana, this is Tracy Doyle and Robin Davisson. You read Tracy's Cantonbury Tale columns in the newspaper," Poppy replied. "She's Robin's cousin. I've told you about Robin. She owns the antique shop I clean."

Robin greeted the older woman with a smile, and Tracy stepped forward. "Merry Christmas, Mrs. McLaren. I brought you a little something." She presented the poinsettia, which the woman accepted with a happy smile.

"How kind. Thank you so much. And please, call me Elaine. Everyone does." Then in a teasing tone, she said, "I hope you purchased this at Fancy Floral. I used to work there." She placed the plant on the corner of the table.

"Yes ma'am, I did," Tracy replied, laughing. "It's a lovely shop."

Elaine smiled rather wistfully. "It always was a pretty place, especially at Christmas and Valentine's Day. I haven't been there in years." She indicated two chairs next to the single bed. "Won't you girls have a seat? Can you stay for a while?" She directed the second question to Poppy.

Poppy draped an arm around her grandmother's shoulders to give her a hug. "We can't stay long, Nana, but Tracy wanted to meet you, and Robin came along." As there were no other chairs to sit in,

137

Poppy plopped down on the edge of her grandmother's bed, which was covered with a log cabin quilt in various shades of green, brown, and cream with coordinating pillow shams.

The room was attractive and homey, with a floor lamp near the card table and a dresser crowded with family photos. Most of them were of Poppy at various ages and a tall, gray-haired man many years older—presumably the late Mr. McLaren. A few small potted succulents were scattered in between the framed photographs.

Elaine adjusted her wheelchair so she could face Tracy more easily. "I can't imagine why you've come to see me, but I'm glad you did. Does it have something to do with your newspaper column?"

Before Tracy could explain, Poppy blurted out, "Tracy wants to know about the Woman in White—about the flowers on the grave."

Elaine raised her eyebrows. She glanced at Robin before fixing Tracy with a penetrating stare. "Why? Are you writing about her?"

Tracy quickly noted that the elderly woman had assumed a more guarded posture. She wished Poppy had let her ease the topic into the conversation. But that couldn't be helped now. She plunged in. "I found an interesting scrapbook in my grandmother's attic, and it has piqued my interest in her." Tracy summarized the scrapbook's contents and her interest in continuing Grandma Pearl's quest for discovering the woman's identity.

Elaine frowned. "Who was your grandmother?"

"Her name was Pearl Wallace Allen," Robin volunteered. "Perhaps you knew her?"

"Why, yes, I did, but not personally. She was a frequent customer at the shop." Her frown deepened. "I wonder why she was so interested in that young woman. Were they related in some way? Is that why she kept a scrapbook?" She seemed mildly astonished by the possibility.

"According to my neighbor Columbia Burke, who was a close friend of my grandmother's before she died, Grandma Pearl longed to find the woman's relatives or at least a friend so that her identity could be revealed. She didn't like the idea that someone could leave this world without a name, without someone caring."

Elaine laced her fingers together in her lap. In a sharp tone, she said, "Obviously, someone did care, or they wouldn't have ordered flowers for her grave year after year."

Tracy nodded. "Poppy told me that she accompanied you once to the cemetery to place flowers on the woman's grave."

With a disapproving glance in Poppy's direction, Elaine nodded. "Once."

"Can you tell us who ordered those flowers? White roses, weren't they?" Robin asked.

"I can't say." Elaine closed her mouth in firm lines.

"You can't, or won't?" Tracy asked in a coaxing tone. Mustering a warm, teasing smile, she added, "As far as I know, there's no florist-customer privilege like doctors and patients have. You won't be breaking any laws by telling me. It was such a long time ago. How can it matter now?"

Elaine replied, "To my way of thinking, we should let sleeping dogs lie."

"Oh, Nana," Poppy protested. She'd been silent up to now but seemed determined to help Tracy get the information she sought. "No one will care. You can tell."

Elaine turned her head to look out the window. Tracy followed her gaze. Outside, the late afternoon sun had sunk low in the sky. A windbreak of trees blocked the view of the street beyond. Long shadows appeared across the window as though they tried to peek into the room.

"Could you at least tell us why the customer bought the flowers?" Robin pleaded. "Was he or she a family member? An acquaintance? Or maybe just a kind and thoughtful benefactor who never knew her? Our grandmother was concerned that no one ever stepped up to give the young woman a name."

"I can't say," Elaine repeated. She hunched lower in the wheelchair as though wishing to shrink from view. "But it wasn't your grandmother, if that's what you really want to know."

"Perhaps it was a lover—a married man too embarrassed to admit that he and the young woman were having an illicit relationship," Tracy pressed.

"I'm not going to tell, so there's no use asking me any further questions." Elaine crossed her arms. To Tracy, it appeared as though Poppy's grandmother was wrapping the secret around herself like a kind of shawl or blanket, holding it tight and close to her chest. Tracy knew without a doubt that no matter how she might pry or push, this woman would not yield. Was the secret that important? Had Elaine made a long-ago promise she intended to keep?

Tracy glanced at Poppy, who sat slumped on the edge of the bed looking rather embarrassed. Her cheeks were flushed, and she was frowning. She seemed perplexed by her grandmother's reticence. "Oh, c'mon, Nana, spill the beans. After all this time, what difference could it possibly make?"

The Cameo Clue

"Gwen Montgomery, the new owner of the flower shop, told me that no one has ordered flowers for the grave for the past several years," Tracy said. "Whoever was keeping up the long-held tradition has now stopped."

Elaine uncrossed her arms and made a fidgety gesture with her hands. "I'd like to see your grandmother's scrapbook sometime."

"I'd be happy to show it to you," Tracy told her and meant it. Maybe seeing the scrapbook and the cameo brooch would prompt the elderly woman to share a small portion of what she knew. But no secrets would be revealed today. Some clams were harder to pry open than others. Accepting her sullen reluctance as a kind of dismissal, Tracy rose from her chair. Robin did the same. Poppy, taking her cue from them, slid off the bed. She gave her grandmother a kiss on the cheek and told her she'd see her soon.

"Thank you for speaking with us, Elaine," Tracy said. "I'll stop by with the scrapbook. I think you'll find it very interesting."

"Thank you for the poinsettia," Elaine said, giving Tracy a wan smile and a warmer one for Robin.

"You're most welcome." When Tracy reached the door, she turned and said, "I'll return soon."

Elaine nodded. "Yes, please do that. I'm sorry I can't give you the information you want. But you see, it's not my secret to share."

Not her secret to share? Tracy wondered if Elaine McLaren might in some way be related to the mysterious stranger now buried without a name in the cemetery.

Poppy wrung her hands as they walked down the corridor. "I'm so sorry, Tracy. I didn't realize the whole white rose thing was so top secret. That mysterious young woman has been dead a long time.

141

SECRETS FROM GRANDMA'S ATTIC

What difference does it make who ordered the flowers for her grave?"

Tracy shrugged. "No need to apologize, Poppy. I am disappointed, I'll admit that. I was hoping your grandmother would confide in me. Instead, the whole incident is more mysterious than ever."

"I'm certainly intrigued," Robin put in.

"Did you mean it when you said you'd come back and bring the scrapbook?" Poppy asked Tracy.

"Yes, I intend to. I may even do it tomorrow. Strike while the iron is hot, Grandma Pearl used to say."

As they reached the entrance, the double doors opened wide. Eric Watson plowed through, a gust of wind following him. Tracy stared at him. Eric, here? He froze, his startled gaze darting from Tracy and Robin to Poppy and back again to Tracy.

"What are you doing here?" His voice sounded gruff and tinged with surprise.

Tracy arched an eyebrow. "I've been visiting Poppy's grandmother." She tipped her head toward her friend. "Poppy Maldonado, this is the editor-in-chief of the *Lewis County Times*, Eric Watson. Eric, I believe you've already met my cousin Robin."

"Merry Christmas," Poppy said in her usual cheery voice. But the slight frown between her eyes revealed to Tracy that she'd been slightly put off by Eric's bluntness.

"Sure, right, Merry Christmas." Eric's cheeks flushed. With embarrassment? Or from the cold? He held the door for them, casting Tracy one last quizzical frown as she passed him.

"What a grump," Robin muttered as they hurried down the sidewalk to Tracy's vehicle.

The Cameo Clue

Poppy asked, "Is he always so rude?"

"Only lately," Tracy said. As she recalled the somewhat harried look in Eric's eyes when he'd given her that one last glance, Tracy couldn't help thinking it had nothing to do with a rejection letter.

Was it anxiety? Fear?

Maybe it was.

But fear of what? Or who?

September 20, 1944
Oaklawn Retreat

Dear Aunt Violet,

I received your letter yesterday. I can't tell you how excited I was. Why, I was fairly over the moon! I read it four or five times. I was that thrilled to receive it. I even read it to the other women in the ward. Thank you, thank you for writing. However, I must confess I am disappointed that you and Uncle Alfred will not be able to come see me. I realize it's quite a distance. I'd forgotten too about gasoline being rationed. Since I don't drive or own a car, it just never entered my mind. I'm disappointed, but I understand. The war has changed everything, hasn't it? What is that saying? These are the times that try men's souls.

Until I received your letter, I'd been feeling pretty low. Another patient in the ward died. She was there in the morning, although she never touched her breakfast tray. She was gone by suppertime. Lost her battle, the nurse told us.

Passed away.

Deceased.

Is that to be my grim future? I shudder to think about it. Sometimes I'm terrified that I'm losing my battle with TB too.

As you may guess by now, the highlight of each day is when they deliver mail. I had a letter this past week from Mrs. Batterson too—you remember my mentioning her, don't you? She used to be my landlady. She moved the few things I left at her place into the attic because Jilly brought home another girl to share the room.

Mrs. B said there's no rush for claiming my belongings, but she hinted that it would be best for me to make other living arrangements when I'm released from the sanatorium—whenever that may be. My heart sinks when I think about how long I've been here and how long I may have to continue to stay. Some days it feels like I'll be here forever. There's a man who has been a patient for nearly a year. A whole year!

The best day of the week is Sunday, when families come to visit. Everyone seems much more cheerful on Sundays, even those of us who don't get visitors. I guess maybe cheerfulness is contagious—like TB, but in a nice way. Or maybe it's the home-baked goodies that some of the visitors bring. Mona's mother came this past weekend for the first time and brought a layer cake—devil's food. Used up all her sugar ration, I'll bet, but it was delicious!

Mona's mother is a cheerful soul. I like her a lot. Mona was so happy to see her. They chatted about what was going on back in Bloomington—that's where Mona's from. I listened in, of course. Everything they talked about seemed more interesting than what goes on here—even their next-door neighbor's goiter operation! They joked and laughed, and I must say the visit did Mona a world of good and me too.

Did I mention that the nurses cut off Mona's braids? Her hair is short now, like a boy's. It's supposed to help keep the fevers down, they told her, but they haven't cut my hair yet.

The new patient in the bed across from mine had a visitor too. Her daughter, a young woman in her twenties with bright red hair. A real carrottop. She unthinkingly picked up her mother's glass of milk from the bedside table and drank from it. The floor nurse happened to see her and ran over shrieking, "What on earth are you doing? Don't you know you can catch TB?" The nurse snatched the glass from her and took it away—to the kitchen, I presume.

I got to thinking about that incident later, and I suppose that's why Mrs. B doesn't want me to come back and live at her place. I think everyone's a little scared about TB and how contagious it is. I suppose she thinks I might contaminate a glass or cup when I drink from it, even if the doctors say I'm cured. I don't know.

Of course, a lot of us here have no visitors because folks are afraid of catching what we have. Nurse Booth explained that the fear of TB is at a fever pitch, and folks who are on the scrawny side or sickly, with ear infections and bronchitis and that sort of thing, are considered highly susceptible to the disease.

My routine hasn't changed much. I'm still enduring lots of tests. They cram tubes down my throat some days, and there are routine spinal taps and endless sputum jars. One of the doctors gave me a shot in my behind. He said they are experimenting with new treatments and hoping to find a cure for TB real soon—one that won't take months and months or even years.

There are days when I feel I may never get better, that I may die here. Nurse Booth says I mustn't have a bleak outlook just because the prognosis based on my X-rays isn't so good. My sputum is still testing positive for the TB germ—Nurse Booth calls it bacillus—so I guess I'm not getting better even though I feel a little stronger and am gaining some weight back.

During rest periods, I'm still expected to lie flat much of the time. Even activities such as reading or writing letters are not allowed when I'm supposed to be in the full resting position. All of us patients are expected to be in bed from nine at night until six in the morning. I think I mentioned that before. That's the routine, and they stick to it. Combining this with the four hours of rest during the day means that we're in bed a lot, but not as much as before. Still, I feel like such a slug. So much time on my hands. I'm sorry if I've written about all this before. You must find my letters so boring, but my life is not very exciting.

Sometimes, if we're not running a temperature, we are allowed to get up to play cards or checkers with one another. I like playing pinochle and hearts. Of course, we do this on the screened porch. Fresh air and sunshine, don't you know? Do you and Dory play any games together? Does Uncle Alfred play chess or checkers? Could you write and tell me about the sort of things you do for fun?

Did I tell you we have a library here with all sorts of books—adventure, detective, historical, autobiographies, and even scientific? The library is quite extensive, or so I'm told—as well stocked as any small-town library. They say the books were donated by local schools and libraries. Those of us not allowed to walk down that way can get any book we want from the woman who comes through the wards with a mobile book cart. I like to read magazines mostly, especially The Saturday Evening Post *and* Life. *Keeps me up on current world news. And the war reports, of course.*

Everyone talks about the war—even in this isolated place. Makes my stomach churn to hear of all the big battles and so many soldiers dying. Most people here don't know I'm a widow, that my Tom died in action. My heart still clutches in my chest sometimes when I think about him, that I'm never going to see him again. But I don't want anyone to feel sorry for me because of that. I feel sorry enough for myself most days.

Guess what? Someone donated a bunch of ukuleles to the san. Can you imagine? Those patients who are musically inclined and allowed to sit up or move around the wards have formed a sort of ukulele band. It's quite funny really. Several of them strolled into our room the other day to serenade us with a lively rendition of "Don't Sit Under the Apple Tree." I couldn't help chuckling. Who knows? I may join the band one day even though I don't know how to play any instrument at all.

I'd better finish this up so it can go out in the afternoon mail. It's almost rest time again. I'll lie flat on my back with one skinny pillow and stare at the ceiling and try not to fret too much. Sometimes I try to pray, and I start off with the best intentions. Then I fall asleep. I hope the Lord isn't too disappointed in my efforts. I'm such a slacker.

Please write soon. Maybe Dory could write me a letter too. I would love to hear from her and find out what she's doing in school and who her friends are and what kind of things she likes to do. I promise to write her back.

Have you given much thought to me coming to stay with you when I am released from here? Have you talked about it

The Cameo Clue

at all? It would only be for a little while. I don't want to mooch off you any longer than can be helped. I just need a soft place to land. Let me know, okay? It would ease my worrying considerably.

    Love to all,

    Trula

Chapter Sixteen

Tracy returned home to whip up a quick spaghetti sauce using marinara from a jar and adding ground beef, onions, and button mushrooms. She kept recalling the astonished expression on Eric's face when he ran into her and Poppy leaving the nursing home. There was no mistaking his surprise, which meant he had not followed her there. He had not expected to see Tracy exiting the building. But then, she'd not expected to see him there either. Was it possible that his mother lived in the same nursing home as Elaine McLaren? Tracy had been under the impression that Mrs. Watson still lived at home or perhaps with one of Eric's sisters. She could be mistaken, of course. Perhaps she could ask Eric by way of a friendly conversation.

She pondered too what Poppy's grandmother meant when she'd said *It's not my secret to share*. Then whose secret was it? If Elaine was telling the truth—and Tracy had no reason to suppose that she wasn't—that ruled out the possibility that she was the one responsible for purchasing the white roses and placing them on the grave. Of course, she would have been a child when the first bouquets were secretly taken to the cemetery, but she could have carried on the tradition afterwards. If so, why? Who was she protecting? Her parents—Poppy's great-grandparents? It was all such a muddle. Tracy felt more confused than ever.

The Cameo Clue

"Smells delicious," Jeff said when he arrived home. Sadie greeted him with a high-pitched bark and a great deal of energetic tail wagging. Tracy greeted him with a kiss. Jeff held his briefcase in one hand and pulled her close with the other, wrapping her in a one-armed hug. Tracy felt immensely blessed to have Jeff as her husband.

She led him to the kitchen where he took a seat at the small table in the corner. While they dined, Tracy told him about her day. Crunching his way through a hefty slice of garlic toast, Jeff listened carefully. Every now and then he'd raise his eyebrows and give a grunt of understanding. When she finished, he said, "If we knew why the flowers were placed on the grave each year, that might help us figure out who the woman was."

Shaking her head, Tracy countered, "I don't think so. A sympathetic person could have made the gesture purely out of kindness. In fact, it's just the sort of thing Grandma Pearl might have done. Elaine did say my grandmother was a regular customer, but not the one who purchased the roses for the grave."

Jeff scooped a forkful of noodles into his mouth and chased them down with a gulp of water. "Why bother to keep the bouquet so hush-hush?"

"Your guess is as good as mine," Tracy said. "The woman who now owns Fancy Floral did mention that no one has placed an order for a special white rose bouquet in the past five years. And guess who arrived at the nursing home just as Poppy, Robin, and I were leaving?" She speared a mushroom and watched Jeff's expression as she announced, "Eric Watson."

"What?" Jeff frowned. "Did he follow you there? You said he's been acting squirrelly lately."

"No, I don't think he followed me there. He appeared quite surprised to see me. I was surprised to see him there too. I'm wondering if his mother lives there, or someone else he knows." Tracy wondered too if that might account for Eric's behavior. Maybe someone he cared about was having serious health issues.

"You look a little frazzled, honey," Jeff said as he leaned back in his chair. His eyes revealed his concern.

"It's been a long day, and I'm tired," she said with a sigh. "The pieces of this puzzle are constantly swirling around in my mind. I can't seem to find a corner piece to begin building the border."

Jeff reached over to squeeze her hand. "You know, Tracy, I'm beginning to wonder if Columbia was right after all. Maybe you should leave this Woman in White thing well enough alone. Some people do keep skeletons in their closet and usually prefer to leave them there, away from public scrutiny."

"Elaine McLaren said something along those same lines," Tracy replied. She dabbed the corner of her mouth with a napkin. "Let sleeping dogs lie—that's how she put it. Aunt Ruth too. Perhaps they're worried about someone's reputation being smeared."

"That might be the wisest thing to do," Jeff suggested. "Even your grandmother dropped her pursuit somewhere along the line. She either decided it wasn't important or that it was hopeless."

"But it doesn't mean she lost interest," Tracy pointed out. "She wrote letters to hospitals trying to find out if they had a recent TB patient fitting the young woman's description—perhaps one who left against doctors' orders."

The Cameo Clue

Jeff pointed his fork at her. "You said the woman died from tuberculosis, right?"

"She had tuberculosis, but she may have died from pneumonia or some other complication," Tracy said. "I'll have to double-check the articles that mentioned the doctor's report."

"I wonder if Grandma Pearl contacted the Missouri TB sanatorium over in Mount Vernon. The mysterious woman might have been a patient there."

Tracy's interest was piqued. "I didn't realize we have a TB sanatorium in our state."

"It closed back in the 1970s because of new treatments for tuberculosis," Jeff said. "The University of Missouri uses the buildings now for something or other, I think."

"What's the difference between a sanitarium and a sanatorium?"

"Good question." Jeff took another bite of his spaghetti. "I honestly don't know. You'll have to look it up."

"I will. Perhaps Grandma Pearl did contact the sanatorium. But without a list of who she sent letters to, I can't follow up or pick up where she left off." Tracy paused, frowning. "I wonder why she didn't save the response letters she received from the hospitals she contacted. She could have put them in the scrapbook along with that cameo brooch."

"There was no need to," Jeff replied, slipping a morsel of garlic bread to Sadie under the table. "If the responses were negative, that a young woman matching the police sketch had not been a patient there, why keep those letters?"

Tracy shrugged. "I suppose you're right. Why bother?" Tracy wondered—not for the first time—if her own search would prove as fruitless as her grandmother's had been. Maybe she should throw in the towel. Was it really worth pursuing the matter? The nameless young woman had been given a Christian burial nearly eighty years ago. What difference could it make now if anyone learned her name or not?

After supper, Jeff retreated to his home office to grade papers. It was that time of year when end-of-the-semester assignments came due, and he had a pile to wade through. Tracy loaded the dishwasher and tidied the kitchen. She really needed to tackle the remainder of her Christmas cards. She and Jeff had received several from friends and family, like Aunt Abigail, who lived out of town, and Tracy wanted to return the favor.

She also needed to wrap the Christmas tree ornaments she'd purchased for each of her grandchildren. It was a custom she'd started when the first one was born. This year there would be a special "Baby's First Christmas" ornament for Chad and Anna's infant daughter, Elizabeth Pearl. Tracy planned to continue the custom until each one graduated from high school. One day all of her grandchildren would have eighteen ornaments to place on their Christmas trees when they had homes of their own.

As she rummaged for the postage stamps, her cell phone rang. It was Amy. She swiped the screen and held the phone to her ear. "Hey, Sis, what are you up to? Long day at school?"

"Smooth sailing today for a change," Amy replied. "I wanted to thank you again for the rocking chair and for coming to the shower."

"I knew you'd love it."

"I do," Amy said, "but it was so expensive. You shouldn't have."

"Hey, you're my only sister, and you're getting married to the love of your life. Such occasions call for special presents," Tracy told her.

The Cameo Clue

"I also want to thank you for talking with Jana the other day," Amy continued. "I don't know what you said, but there have been no tantrums and no tears since then."

"I'm glad to hear it," Tracy said. "Jana and Matt have been through a lot in their young lives. Change is hard for most people, perhaps even more so for the two of them. They've just come through a complicated adoption process and finally feel settled comfortably and securely in your home. Now they'll be moving out and starting over again in a new house with new family members to adjust to. Jana might be feeling a little insecure."

"Perhaps," Amy said. "I hope that's all it is. I'll have to reassure her that this change will be a happy one—for all of us." She sighed heavily. "So how are you coming along with Grandma Pearl's scrapbook mystery?"

This time Tracy sighed. "It's still very mysterious. Maybe more so than before."

"No luck finding a name for the Woman in White?"

"Not yet," Tracy said. "But I had an interesting conversation with Pastor Gary and one with an elderly woman who once worked in the floral shop where the white roses were purchased." Tracy summarized these visits and shared what she'd learned so far. "It turns out that Elaine McLaren is Poppy's grandmother. She knows who ordered the flowers for the grave, but she won't spill the beans."

"What? How old is the woman, for heaven's sake?" Amy's tone was incredulous. "She must be ancient. Didn't all this happen in the 1940s?"

"Elaine is in her late eighties. Still spry and determined not to share what she knows. But you're right—this secret has been passed

SECRETS FROM GRANDMA'S ATTIC

down from one generation to another. She would have been a kid back in 1944. Still, she's the key to the mystery. I'm sure of that. I feel it in my bones."

There was a slight pause before Amy asked, "Does it really matter after all this time? Maybe you should just let the nameless woman rest in peace."

Tracy remained silent. Hadn't she had the same misgivings a short while ago? Then she recalled the thoughts and feelings she'd had while standing beside the young woman's grave. If someone had made the gesture of remembering her with flowers simply out of kindness, why not admit it? What could be the harm? But the biggest mystery—the one that perplexed Tracy the most—was why, if someone knew the woman's name, had they never stepped forward to say so?

Chapter Seventeen

*T*racy headed to the nursing home first thing Friday morning, scrapbook in hand. She'd bundled up in a coat, scarf, and lined gloves, but the cold was intense enough to penetrate her clothes, chilling her to the bone. If the weather continued to get colder like this, they might just have snow for Christmas after all.

As she signed in at the front desk, Tracy experienced a surge of optimism. She felt certain that Elaine McLaren, when she looked through the scrapbook Grandma Pearl had kept so diligently, would no longer believe Tracy was merely a curiosity seeker or a busybody attempting to pry into secrets from the past. No, she was on a truth-finding mission.

"I think Mrs. McLaren is still in the dining room," the young attendant told her. Her long bangs were streaked red and white, reminding Tracy of peppermint. "If she isn't there, she'll be in her room. Number 106."

Hugging the scrapbook to her chest, Tracy followed the young woman's directions, strolling down the corridor to the sunny dining room. She could hear Christmas carols playing faintly in the background. Sure enough, she found Poppy's grandmother lingering over coffee and laughing with two other elderly women, presumably

SECRETS FROM GRANDMA'S ATTIC

residents too. Elaine seemed mildly startled when she glanced up and noticed Tracy hovering at her elbow.

"Good morning, Mrs. McLaren. I'm Tracy Doyle. We met yesterday when I came with Poppy."

In a slightly irritated tone, Elaine responded, "Of course I remember you. I'm not in my dotage yet." She fixed her blue eyes on the scrapbook. "And I thought I told you to call me Elaine."

The two other women rose and left, promising to see Elaine later. Elaine didn't bother to introduce them, and Tracy sensed the elderly woman was annoyed. But why? Yesterday, she'd told Tracy she'd like to see the scrapbook. Well, here she was, scrapbook in hand. Make hay while the sun shines, her grandparents always said. That was just what she was doing.

Tracy placed the scrapbook on the table in front of Elaine and then sat down in one of the chairs across from her. "Here's my grandmother's scrapbook. I promised I'd show it to you."

"Let's go look at it in my room," Elaine suggested. She placed the scrapbook on her lap and spun her motorized wheelchair around. Tracy stood up and followed the woman to her room. Everything appeared just as it had yesterday. The poinsettia Tracy had given her took pride of place in the center of the low dresser. Tracy returned to the same chair she'd sat in yesterday and watched Elaine open the scrapbook. She turned the stiff pages slowly, appearing to read some of the articles carefully. Others, she simply skimmed. Once she raised her gaze to meet Tracy's then dropped her eyes back to the open page.

"I don't understand why you're probing into this," Elaine murmured. "It's ancient history." She tucked a strand of snowy white hair behind her ear. Tracy noted that Elaine wore a different pair of

The Cameo Clue

dangling earrings today—tiny green wreaths festooned with even tinier red bows. Cute and Christmassy.

"True, but the incident meant something to my grandmother. I don't know why. At one time, she wanted me to look into the matter. She may have changed her mind before she passed away. Frankly, I don't know." Tracy lifted her shoulder in a shrug.

Elaine pointed to the police sketch of the unknown woman. "She was young, wasn't she?"

Tracy agreed. Hoping to tempt Elaine into revealing information, she asked, "Did you ever meet her? Was she a Canton resident? You would have been a child, I know, but it would be hard not to remember someone who died so suddenly, I think."

"I was only ten back in 1944. No, I never met her. And that's the honest truth. Besides, she died almost immediately after arriving in Canton." Elaine shot Tracy a challenging stare. After a prolonged silence, she added almost reluctantly, "But I will say this much. This sketch." She tapped the picture with a thin finger. "It's a good likeness."

Tracy arched an eyebrow. "How would you know, if you never met her?"

Elaine hesitated before replying, "I once saw a photo of her."

"A photo in a newspaper?"

"A wedding photo. In a picture frame," Elaine replied.

"Then you do know who she is!" Tracy's tone was both triumphant and accusatory.

"No, I don't know her name. Someone may have mentioned it once, a long time ago, but I don't remember, and that's the truth. I'm not as young as I used to be," Elaine said rather gruffly. "And don't ask me where I saw the photo, because I'm not telling." She gave Tracy a curt nod. "I've already said more than enough."

Musing out loud, Tracy said, "So the person who shared the photo with you may have been the same person who purchased the white roses. Am I right?"

With a fierce frown, Elaine snapped, "Who said anyone showed me the photo? Maybe I just happened to notice it on a desk or hanging on a wall or propped on a mantelpiece. I don't remember exactly."

"Here in Canton?" Tracy pressed.

Elaine swallowed hard. "I'm not saying. I simply can't." She turned a troubled gaze on Tracy's face. "If I did, it would be a betrayal of sorts. I wish you'd just drop it before someone gets hurt. Please."

"You're not going to tell me anything else, are you?" Realizing this, Tracy slumped in her chair.

"I can't. Like I said, it's not my secret to tell. And if you keep digging into this affair, you might end up hurting someone, and I don't think you want to do that."

Tracy said, "Someone still living." It was a statement not a question. The dead were beyond being hurt, so Elaine must have a living, breathing person in mind.

After a moment or two, Tracy tried a different approach. "Okay, I won't badger you anymore. Keep your secret if you must. I already know more than I did when I first started out, and I feel certain I'm going to eventually discover the name of this young woman."

"What do you think you know?" Elaine demanded.

"For one thing, you told me that my grandmother is not the one who bought the flowers or put them on her grave. Secondly, I know

The Cameo Clue

the tradition of placing the roses on the grave extends through generations—at least two, and maybe even three."

"How do you know that?"

Tracy sighed. "As you just pointed out, you were a child in 1944. Someone bought the flowers and placed them on the grave each year long before you were an employee at the floral shop. This went on for years—decades. When you became an adult, you took the orders for the white roses. At first, I considered the possibility that you carried on the tradition once the first customer died, but I've changed my mind. I think you would have told me if it was you. But you haven't. You're protecting someone else. Why, I don't know."

Elaine fixed her with a blank stare. Tracy continued. "Presumably, it's someone here in Canton, someone you've known for years. Someone you care about."

Elain slammed the scrapbook shut and thrust it toward her. "You need to leave this alone."

Behind the woman's angry glare, Tracy thought she saw a hint of fear. What was Elaine McLaren so afraid of?

Just then Tracy's cell buzzed. It seemed particularly loud in the silence that followed Elaine's statement. "Excuse me," Tracy said, reaching into her purse. It was a text from Lincoln Bailey. FOUND THE SUITCASE! Tracy's heart leaped with joy. She quickly texted back, MEET YOU AT YOUR OFFICE.

Lincoln sent a thumbs-up emoji in response.

Tracy rose, slipping her purse strap over her shoulder and tucking the scrapbook under one arm. "Thank you for your time, Elaine. I'm sorry if this has been painful. I didn't mean for it to be. But I believe that the poor woman laid to rest in our cemetery deserves to be known by her name, no matter how unpleasant that may prove for someone else. I won't bother you any further. I just wish you could trust me enough to tell me what you know. Perhaps the fact that I work for the local newspaper has made you leery. Perhaps you think I'm after a scoop or some sensational story that might embarrass you or someone you care about. That's the furthest thing from the truth, believe me."

As she took hold of the doorknob, preparing to leave the room, Tracy turned, reaching into her purse. "If you change your mind and want to talk, you can reach me at either of these numbers." She gave Elaine a business card with both her personal cell number and the office number.

Then she made one last parting attempt. "By the way, I have the cameo brooch—the one the woman is wearing in that sketch. It appears to be a family heirloom. Someone may want it back someday."

Elaine's eyes widened, but she said nothing, not even goodbye. Tracy didn't fret about it though. She hurried to her car, so excited about the text from Lincoln that she barely felt the cold nipping her nose and cheeks.

Against all odds, Lincoln had found the suitcase! Her thoughts ping-ponged between that exciting news and the intriguing tidbit Elaine had shared. She'd once seen a photo of the Woman in White. A wedding photo. A framed photograph—not a missing person's poster or a picture in a wallet or a newspaper photograph. And if this photo was on display in someone's home or office, why hadn't anyone else in town noticed?

Tracy guessed that Elaine had seen the photo here in Canton. That would explain why the sick young woman had arrived in town

The Cameo Clue

by bus. She was indeed coming to visit someone who lived here. She'd not been passing through as the police had once conjectured. Nor had she disembarked because she felt poorly and wanted to see a doctor. She'd intended to come to Canton all along. Why, then, had no one in Canton come forward to identify her, to claim her as their long-lost sister, daughter, wife, or mother?

Tracy also ruled out the probability that the Woman in White had come to Canton to meet a lover. She was a married woman or perhaps a widow—even a war widow. If she'd been "the other woman" from out of town, she wouldn't be in a wedding photograph in Canton. It was looking more and more like she had come to visit a relative who lived in town. Someone who was close enough to her to have her wedding picture in their home.

When she got to the top of the stairs that led to his office, Lincoln waved her in through the open door.

"I can't believe you found the suitcase," Tracy gasped. Between the cold air outside and the exertion from dashing up the stairs, she needed to catch her breath.

"I didn't find it," Lincoln said. "The credit goes to Danica Jones, who works at the county building. She's been reorganizing things and recalled seeing an old suitcase in a storage closet several months ago. When I came along making inquiries, she knew just where it was, and she's happy to be rid of it. There it is."

Lincoln pointed to an office chair against the wall. The suitcase was somewhat battered and dusty, the leather worn, the wooden handle cracked. Tracy could hardly believe their good luck. She made a silent vow to make a batch of fudge for Danica Jones. "Have you opened it yet?"

163

SECRETS FROM GRANDMA'S ATTIC

"No." Lincoln smiled. "I thought I'd let you have the honor. Open it here on my desk." He stepped aside, allowing her room to place the small suitcase on the desk blotter. Just as Tracy clicked the latches, Melody bustled through the open door of her husband's office, pausing breathlessly just inside the room. Her dark eyes sparkled with bright anticipation.

"Have you opened it yet?"

Tracy laughed. "You're just in time. I'm going to do that now. How'd you know Lincoln found it?"

Unwrapping the blue scarf from around her neck and dropping it onto a chair, Melody said, "Lincoln sent me a text. I've been keen on learning more about the Woman in White. I haven't been able to get her out of my mind since we spoke about her the other day. I can hardly believe Danica found the old thing. Why it wasn't tossed out years ago, I just don't know."

"Lucky for us," Tracy said, smiling broadly. Turning to Lincoln, she asked, "Do I need to sign anything? Some sort of official form to make this legal?"

Lincoln shook his head. "The suitcase is not evidence of a crime or anything of that nature. And even if it had been, the statute of limitations would have expired by now. There's really no reason in the world that the police or the county officials or any other agency kept possession of it all this time. It's yours if you want it."

Tracy glanced from Lincoln's smiling face to Melody's eager one. "Well, here goes."

She lifted the lid.

The Cameo Clue

October 1, 1944
Oaklawn Retreat

Dear Aunt Vi,

I've had no letter again from you in such a long while. Is everything okay? When I don't hear from you, I worry. I imagine all sorts of bad things happening where you are. I saw in the newspaper that a munitions factory somewhere near Lake Michigan blew up. People died. They are wondering if it was sabotage. I hope there are no munitions factories near Canton where you live.

It's getting chilly here, especially at night, but they still expect us to sit outside to get our daily dose of fresh air and sunshine. The porch is now decorated with pumpkins and a make-believe scarecrow at one end. It's kind of festive. We still sleep with the windows wide open at night too. I asked for an extra blanket because it can be so cold, especially when it's blustery outside.

Can't imagine how miserable it will be trying to sleep in the wards come winter if they still keep the windows open. I'll have to ask for three extra blankets!

I do have good news to share, and that's why I'm writing to you. I'm putting on weight! That's no surprise, I suppose, since all I do is eat and lie around like a log. But the nurse assures me this is a sign that I'm getting healthy again. So I'll keep eating everything on my tray and drinking all my hot cocoa. I'm really so tickled about it.

I had another short letter from my friend Jilly back at Mrs. Batterson's boardinghouse in Peoria. She said that Mr. Meslin, who owns the theater where I used to work, lost his only son recently. The poor boy was killed in action, just like my Tom. Mr. Meslin put a gold star in the window of the box office at the theater. He was so proud that his Herbie was serving in Europe. Italy maybe. I located it once on a map. He'd been fighting Nazis and their Italian allies. I guess the Nazis are everywhere now. The boy couldn't have been more than nineteen when he signed up. Now he's gone. Poor Mr. and Mrs. Meslin must be beside themselves with grief. He was their only child.

Jilly says there are more and more gold star families in Peoria now—families who have lost sons and husbands in the war. She says you can see blue stars and gold stars in the windows of most of the houses on the street. She says I'm a gold star widow. I guess I am. I hadn't thought about that before. Sometimes I can't believe that my Tom is never going to come home. Maybe the war department made a mistake. Maybe he's not really dead but just a prisoner somewhere. Maybe they got Tom confused with someone else. Do you think that's possible?

The doctors check on my progress several times a week. Dr. Spooner says I'm not getting better fast enough even though I'm gaining some weight back. Nurse Fanny Booth said I mustn't worry about it. She says worry will prevent me from getting better. Sometimes she forces me to drink some kind of medicine, and then I have to swallow something the size of a caramel candy with a plastic tube attached to one end. They don't give me anything for the pain. It feels dreadful when it goes down, like it's tearing up my throat. It hurts. Between the treatments and the disease, I'm in pain most of the time. My chest still hurts. But I remind myself there are other patients worse off than me and I'm living in a comfortable place where people are taking good care of me. I'm not going to complain. I can read all the books and magazines I want. Jilly says I should enjoy being spoiled for a while.

Please write, Aunt Vi. I live for letters. Could Dory Dearie write too?

Love,

Your only niece,

Trula

Chapter Eighteen

A faint whiff of lavender tickled Tracy's nose when she opened the suitcase. Melody hovered at her elbow watching as Tracy removed one item after the next. First was a small clutch purse. It contained nothing more than a few old dollar bills, some change, a couple of handkerchiefs, a tube of bright red lipstick, and a comb. Nothing with the woman's name on it. No ration card. No driver's license.

Everything else had been neatly folded. The white wool coat, two long-sleeved wool dresses with matching fabric-covered skinny belts, a cardigan, nylon stockings, undergarments, bedroom slippers, and a pair of light blue flannel pajamas with a matching robe. Everything appeared flattened, heavily creased with age, and slightly moth-eaten. Tracy doubted the garments could ever be used again.

"Those look rather institutional," Melody noted, indicating the robe and pajamas. "The sort they hand out in hospitals."

"Or sanatoriums," Tracy added.

"Makes sense," Lincoln said, "considering the doctor's report."

Tracy continued to remove items from the suitcase, placing them on Lincoln's massive desk. Besides the clothing, there wasn't all that much. A small jar of Woodbury face cream, a toothbrush, and a tube of Pepsodent toothpaste. "Hard as a rock," Tracy said,

The Cameo Clue

giving the tube a squeeze. It didn't surprise her. After all, these items had been stashed away for nearly eighty years.

"She traveled light, I'd say," Melody said.

"Nice white coat," Tracy noted. "I'm surprised they didn't bury her with it." At Melody's perplexed expression, she explained. "They dubbed her the Woman in White because when she arrived in Canton on the bus, she was said to be wearing a white dress and this coat."

After Tracy had emptied the suitcase, Lincoln asked, "It that it? Anything else?"

"I don't think so." The two stretchy pouches on either side were empty. Tracy rubbed her hand around the edges and along the seams. She passed the suitcase to Melody, who lifted it and gave it a firm shake.

"Wait, I think I found something." Melody carefully ran her hand across the lining at the bottom. "Look, there's something under here." She gently tugged a piece of blue paper through a tear along the seam. It crackled with age when she unfolded it. "A letter dated November 30, 1944," she said.

Tracy felt a rush of excitement so intense she could barely breathe.

Eyes glowing, Melody read the contents of the letter out loud.

"'Dear Trula, we were happy to receive your letter with the good news about the improvement of your health. It must be difficult living there for such a length of time. I'm sure you miss your friends. I think it would be best if you did not come to see us at this time. I hope you understand. Not until you are completely recovered. Sincerely, Aunt Vi.'"

Tracy reached for the letter, scanning the contents again quickly. Her heart pounded. Trula! Vi! Now they had actual names to work

SECRETS FROM GRANDMA'S ATTIC

with. She felt a tingle of joy. "So Aunt Vi didn't want Trula to come for Christmas, but she came anyway?" She exchanged a puzzled glance with Melody and then looked at Lincoln, hoping he had an explanation.

Lincoln shrugged. "So maybe Aunt Vi changed her mind and wrote another letter later, encouraging Trula to come."

"She sounds like a cold, unsympathetic person," Melody said. "I'm surprised Trula wanted to visit her at all."

"Why did Trula save the letter?" Tracy asked.

"And how did the police miss finding it?" Melody asked. She reached for the letter and examined it again.

"We almost did," Tracy pointed out.

There was silence for a while before Lincoln asked, "Is there an envelope?"

Melody patted the lining of the suitcase. "No, there's nothing else."

"This is puzzling," Tracy mused. "If Trula came here to see her relatives, regardless of whether or not she'd been invited, why didn't Aunt Vi or someone else step forward to identify her when the news with the police sketch was released?"

"Perhaps Aunt Vi and family left town for the holidays and missed all the hoopla?" Lincoln suggested.

Tracy shook her head. "No, that still doesn't explain it. Even if Aunt Vi had been out of town when Trula arrived, the news ran in the papers for months. Sooner or later, the family would have noticed the police sketch, would have learned that the authorities sought the public's help in identifying the young woman."

"That's right," Melody agreed. "And I read where the *Times* sometimes ran an updated story on the anniversary of the incident.

The Cameo Clue

So sooner or later this Aunt Vi person would have seen something about it in the paper."

"And sooner or later she'd wonder why she hadn't received another letter from her niece Trula," Tracy added.

"It's unconscionable," Melody huffed. "I can't think of a good enough reason to let that poor young woman be buried in a nameless grave."

Lincoln folded his arms across his chest. "Sorry, Tracy, that the suitcase didn't turn up anything useful."

"But it did!" Tracy protested. "I now know the young woman's name was Trula. She came to see her Aunt Vi—presumably a woman living here in Canton."

Lincoln shrugged. Melody slowly replaced each item back into the suitcase.

Lincoln stroked his chin. "What's next? How are you going track down a woman named Vi with a niece named Trula? There must be dozens of women living in Canton who went by Vi. That could stand for Vivian, Violet, Vienna, Viola."

"Victoria, Virginia, Violetta," Melody said. "And remember, Aunt Vi would now be deceased."

Tracy refused to be daunted. "None of those are common names, and Trula is very unusual. I just have to link the two names together somehow."

"Okay, let's say you track down this Trula and her aunt. That won't completely solve the mystery," Lincoln pointed out. "It doesn't explain why good old Aunt Vi and the rest of her family—if there were other family members—didn't come forward to identify Trula after she died."

Lost in thought, Tracy chewed the inside of her cheek. Lincoln was right. With Trula deceased and Aunt Vi as well, would anyone still be living who could explain the circumstances that led to the young woman being buried without a name?

"I'll have to cross that bridge when I get to it. First, I need to discover Trula's and Vi's surnames."

Lincoln chuckled. "It might help if you knew what Vi's complete first name is. Where do you plan to start your search?"

"I'll need to give that some thought," Tracy said. "I'm just so excited to have a name to begin with. Trula. The Woman in White's name was Trula."

"I'd love to help. I can go through the membership list at the church, looking for anyone named Vi," Melody offered, her eyes dancing. "I might be able to talk Maureen into helping. I'll even volunteer Erica to help when she comes home at the end of her semester."

Tracy tried not to smile. She imagined that the Baileys' college-aged daughter would have other plans for her Christmas break. Plans that didn't include rummaging through musty old church membership lists.

"If you don't come up with any likely candidates, do you think Maureen would be willing to call secretaries at other churches to ask if we could look through their old membership records?"

"Sure, I can ask," Melody said. "But not all the congregations in town are as old as ours. Remember, we're trying to track down someone who was a church member in 1944."

"But dear old Aunt Vi might not have been a church member at all," Lincoln pointed out. "You might want to go through the census records."

The Cameo Clue

Tracy sighed. "Sure, but we don't have a surname."

She wondered if she should pay Elaine McLaren another visit. She dreaded doing so. Hadn't she told Elaine that she wouldn't bother her again? But the woman might remember a customer or neighbor or someone named Vi. Still, it didn't seem right to go back on her promise. Columbia might remember someone with that name. It was hardly possible that Vi would be alive and well, but maybe she had children or grandchildren or another niece living in Canton. It was worth pursuing.

Lincoln interrupted her thoughts with a throaty chuckle. "I can hear those wheels spinning, Tracy." He made a twirling gesture with his finger.

Tracy laughed. "My mind is churning a mile a minute, I'll admit. This is so exciting. I feel like I can finally sink my teeth into something."

"Might as well get started," Melody said. "There can't have been that many women named Vi with a niece named Trula who suffered with TB and who was probably institutionalized for the disease during the war." She slung her purse over her shoulder. "I'm going to get busy right now. No time like the present." Patting her husband on the arm as she passed him, Melody said, "See you at supper, Linc."

He acknowledged her with a smile.

With all the items back in the suitcase, Tracy closed the lid. "You said I could have this?"

"I don't see why not," Lincoln told her. "But don't return it. Danica would be furious." Then, laughing, he added, "Don't stash it upstairs in Pearl's attic either."

Tracy smiled. "No, I won't do that. I intend to return this to Trula's relatives—when I locate them."

Chapter Nineteen

Tracy brought home burgers and fries for supper that evening and gave Jeff a quick and excited summary regarding the recovery of the old suitcase and, most amazing of all, the undiscovered letter stashed in the lining. Promising to fill him in later on all the details, she kissed him goodbye, gave Sadie an affectionate ear rub, and then headed back out into the cold evening to join Amy and the other pageant organizers at the church to help with a partial dress rehearsal and costume check.

On the way, Tracy couldn't get the image of Trula's face out of her mind—if indeed the young woman who'd once owned that suitcase was Trula. It seemed likely though. Tracy had looked at the sketch in the scrapbook so often, she felt as though she knew the young woman, if only a little. She'd been younger than her own daughter, Sara. The poor girl had been ill. And in pain. One could see evidence of that in the slight frown between her eyebrows, the pinched tightness around her full lips. The sketch artist had certainly paid attention to details provided by witnesses.

The church parking lot was full and the foyer noisy with excited, rambunctious children. A handful of frazzled women tried to get them to stand still so costume adjustments could be made while the youth pastor listened to them recite their lines. The scent of popcorn filled the air. Tracy could hear someone plunking haltingly on the piano in the auditorium. She looked through the open double doors and was surprised to see Jana sitting on the piano stool, playing "Away in a Manger." Tracy wondered briefly if her young niece had a musical solo in the pageant. Amy hadn't mentioned it.

"It's like herding cats," Amy said when Tracy joined her near the long table where a variety of pageant props were arranged. Amy wore a work apron with a long deep pocket over her jeans and sweater. The apron appeared to be stashed with everything from tape and scissors to index cards and markers.

"Organized chaos." Tracy chuckled.

While Amy continued to label each object with a number, Tracy noticed a vaguely familiar item—an old jewelry box spray-painted gold, dusted with glitter, and studded with fake green and red gems.

"Aunt Ruth's?" she asked, pointing.

Amy nodded. "One of the wise men's presents."

"What can I do to help?" Tracy asked.

Amy handed her a blank label and a marker. "Here, put a number on that." She pointed to a large baby doll swaddled in what appeared to be flour sack kitchen towels.

Tracy replied, "Baby Jesus, I presume."

"Yes. We're keeping track of which props go with which child so we can hunt them down after the pageant if necessary. Some of the younger boys have been using the shepherds' staffs to wage lightsaber battles in the fellowship hall. We suspect they may want to keep those after the pageant. Someone will have the responsibility of getting them back."

Chuckling, Tracy did as she was told. "By the way, you'll never guess what I now have in my possession."

Amy regarded her with arched eyebrows.

"The suitcase that belonged to the mysterious Woman in White." Tracy gave her sister a smug smile.

"What?" Amy paused, marker and labels in hand. "How did you find that? Where? It's hard to believe it's still around after all this time."

"Oh, I didn't find it," Tracy replied. She went on to explain how she'd asked for Lincoln Bailey's help and how he in turn had given Danica Jones the dubious task of hunting down the suitcase. "I'm thrilled but can hardly believe it was found."

"That's amazing." Amy shook her head. "I mean, it's old. Really old. Was there a handbag too? Anything that could help with identification?"

"Actually, there was a small purse inside the suitcase, but nothing inside the purse with the woman's name on it—no driver's license, no factory ID or government facility badge, not even a ration card," Tracy said. "That still puzzles me. I thought everyone had a ration card back then." She frowned. "But I suppose if she'd been hospitalized or was a patient in a sanatorium, they may have taken it from her."

"Didn't you say Grandma Pearl contacted hospitals, hoping to discover the woman's identity? Maybe she really was a patient." Amy slapped a label on the inside of a glittering cardboard crown. "Maybe she left without getting the doctors' permission. That would explain why she was still ill when she arrived in Canton."

"The pajamas and robe we found look like the kind they hand out in a medical facility. Melody Bailey thought so too. But the big discovery was the letter. It was written to someone named Trula and signed by a woman named Aunt Vi. So I'm thinking the young woman buried in our cemetery is Trula Something-Or-Other, and she came here to Canton to visit her aunt Vi."

A little boy about four years old dressed in a gray donkey costume darted by. Amy called out in her firmest schoolteacher voice, "No running!" The child jolted to a stop and then proceeded at a slower pace to the fellowship hall. Amy turned back to Tracy. "If that's the case, why didn't this Aunt Vi person identify her niece when she died?"

Tracy raised a finger. "That is still a mystery. And of course we don't have a last name for either Trula or her aunt. There was no envelope in the suitcase. Just the letter, now faded and wrinkled with age."

Just then, Natalie, Miles's daughter, dashed down the hall, stopping abruptly in front of Amy near the prop table. "Mrs. Tubb said to give this to you." She thrust a large toy lamb at Amy. "Isn't it cute? And I get to carry it in the play. She said I could."

"I thought you were supposed to be an angel like Jana," Tracy said, smiling at the girl who would soon become Amy's stepdaughter.

Natalie bounced on her toes. "The costume was too itchy and Mrs. Tubb said we have too many angels and not enough shepherds so I said I'd be a shepherd if I could carry the little lamb and she said yes." Turning to Amy, she asked, "That's okay, right?"

Amy smiled. "If it's okay with Mrs. Tubb, it's okay with me."

"Thank you!" Natalie threw her arms around Amy's waist. Amy hugged her back. "I love you," Natalie declared.

"And I love you too, honey." Amy glanced up at Tracy, who noted the slight misting in her sister's eyes.

A child's loud wail immediately attracted their attention. Tracy turned. There stood Jana, awash in tears, a look of sheer dismay on her wet, red face. Amy disentangled herself from Natalie's embrace and called out, "Jana, what's wrong?"

Touching Amy's sleeve, Tracy replied, "Let me take care of this. You've got work to do." Hurrying forward, Tracy placed her hand on Jana's shoulder. "What's wrong, Jana? Did you pinch your finger in the piano when you lowered the lid?"

Several children and a few women turned toward them, curiosity evident in their expressions. Amy hurried over, with Natalie dogging her heels. Jana shook her head, her glance fixed on Amy and Natalie. She swiped the tears from her cheeks. Tracy, suspecting Jana's tears were not related to a physical injury, made up her mind on the spot to get to the bottom of her niece's problem.

"Hey, sweetie, get your coat. You and I are going out for a treat."

Jana sniffed and gave Tracy a surprised look. Tracy, turning back to catch Amy's attention, mouthed the words, "I've got this."

Amy nodded anxiously and cast Tracy a grateful glance. Her shoulders slumped with apparent relief.

"Where are we going?" Jana asked as Tracy helped bundle her into her coat, making sure Jana put on her mittens and stocking cap.

Tracy didn't answer her until they'd gotten into the car and Jana had buckled up in the back seat. "We're going out for hot fudge sundaes." A glance in the rearview mirror at the astonishment on Jana's face convinced Tracy that this was hardly the answer her niece had been expecting.

"Why?" Jana's tone was suspicious.

The Cameo Clue

"It's been a long-held theory of mine that excellent conversations can be had over hot fudge sundaes. That's what we're going to do. We are going to have a heart-to-heart conversation."

"What does heart-to-heart mean, exactly?" Jana asked, still obviously suspicious. At least she was no longer crying. Her tears had dried up, and she was coming out of the sulking stage.

"It means we talk together openly," Tracy explained. "You're honest with me, and I'm honest with you."

At the ice cream shop next to the Banner Hardware store, Tracy ordered two hot fudge sundaes with the works—whipped cream, cherries, chopped peanuts, and lots of sprinkles. Then at a booth in the back where they were not likely to be overheard, she debated the best way to begin.

Tracy waited until Jana took a bite. The little girl's shoulders relaxed, and the stress of the most recent incident drained from her face. Sending up a silent prayer for guidance, Tracy asked, "So why were you crying at the church just now?"

Jana shrugged. "I don't know."

"Sure you do. You're too embarrassed to talk about it, but we're not leaving until you do," Tracy told her. "We might even have to spend the night in here, you curled up on one side of the booth and me on the other."

Jana's head snapped up. She regarded Tracy curiously. Then she giggled. "We can't sleep in a booth!"

"We won't have to if you tell me what's wrong. Open and honest, remember?" Tracy arched a brow. "Your behavior of late has been..." She paused, searching for the right word. "Well, you haven't been

SECRETS FROM GRANDMA'S ATTIC

your usual happy, bubbly self. I care about you. I want to know what's wrong. I can't help fix it until I know what the problem is. Now, Jana, it's your turn. Open and honest."

She stared at her niece, who kept her gaze fixed on her spoon. Her lower lip quivered. "You're unhappy about something," Tracy prompted.

Jana nodded. "And sad," she added in a small voice.

"Sad about something that happened at church?"

Again, Jana nodded. "Mom hugged Natalie—again. She hugs her a lot now."

Tracy frowned. "That makes you sad? Isn't Natalie your best friend? Soon you'll be sisters, like me and your mom. I'm sure there are times when your mom hugs Matt a lot and now Colton too. She has enough hugs to go around, sweetie. You just have to wait your turn. Don't you want your mom to hug Natalie?"

Jana shook her head. She dipped her spoon into the ice cream and stirred it around.

"It's going to be hard for your mom not to hug the people she cares about. She has a big heart." Tracy caught Jana's eye and smiled. "That means she has a lot of love to share—just as she shares her love with you and Matt."

"At first I didn't mind," Jana said. "But now I think things are going to be bad after the wedding."

"What things?" Tracy pressed. She could feel a frown pinching the skin between her eyes. She tried to keep her expression calm.

The Cameo Clue

Jana placed her elbows on the table. She put down her spoon and turned sad eyes on Tracy. "Everything will be different, and not in a good way, after the wedding."

Tracy leaned forward. "Explain it to me, Jana, I don't understand."

Jana heaved a longer sigh. "Mom loves Dr. Miles now. She wants to make him happy. So she's going to love Natalie and Colton more than me and Matt. That will make Dr. Miles happy. Things are never going to be the same again."

Chapter Twenty

Tracy texted Amy to make sure she was at home before returning Jana there. Then, with a little coaxing and a reassuring hug, Tracy urged her to repeat to Amy what she'd confided to Tracy at the ice cream shop. Amy listened and reassured Jana that she loved her to the moon and back and that nothing would ever change that. After giving her mom a quick hug and a mumbled, "I'm sorry," Jana scampered away to her room to get ready for bed.

"The poor darling." Amy watched Jana leave. "She and the other kids worked so hard to get Miles and me together. And now she seems to need reassurance that everything will be okay."

"She's a good kid," Tracy assured her sister as they huddled together in Amy's small kitchen. "At least now you know what's been bothering her. The hot fudge worked its magic—again."

Amy smiled. "Did you use this particular technique with Chad and Sara when they were little?"

"I sure did. It worked until they got to be teenagers. By then they were onto me." Tracy could feel a grin tugging at the corners of her mouth.

"This is one reason I was reluctant to go out with Miles in the first place," Amy said. "I was afraid Matt and Jana might feel left out or insecure. They seemed so excited at first—pleased with the

The Cameo Clue

success of their parent trap and then by the wedding plans and everything. I guess I should have paid more attention to Jana—and Matt too, just to make sure their attitudes hadn't changed."

"It's time for you to have a sit-down discussion with them," Tracy advised. "Be honest and open with one another. Parenting is never easy, but it's the most worthwhile job in the world."

Amy gave Tracy a heartfelt hug. "Thanks, Sis. You're the best."

The following morning—Saturday—Tracy decided to tackle her mile-long to-do list. Not only did she need to tidy up the house and get ready for Sunday dinner with the family, but she decided to take a cue from Columbia and get some early baking done too. She also wanted to follow the lead from the old letter Melody had discovered in the suitcase.

She called both Aunt Ruth and Aunt Abigail and asked if they knew of anyone in Canton with the name Vi or some version of that name. Aunt Ruth said no. Aunt Abigail said she'd have to think about it.

"No one comes to mind right off the top of my head," she said. She then teased Tracy about being a girl sleuth "just like Nancy Drew on the trail of a new mystery." She laughed. "You were always reading those books when you were a kid."

Tracy smiled. How she'd loved those mysteries as a girl! She'd read every one she could get her hands on—even the Dana Girls and Trixie Belden. When she was ten years old, she considered curling up on her bed with a Nancy Drew mystery and a large, long-lasting Tootsie Roll the height of bliss.

After making her phone calls, running the vacuum, and doing a load of laundry, Tracy whipped up three no-bake peppermint pies for tomorrow's lunch. It was one of the easiest desserts she knew how to make. Peppermint ice cream laced with chocolate syrup and dumped into a ready-made chocolate-cookie crust. No muss, no fuss. It was simple and refreshing. And best of all, it could be made well ahead of time and stored in the freezer.

Tracy also made a batch of mocha fudge and, as she did so, her mind flickered back and forth between her to-do list and her interest in tracking down surnames for Trula and Aunt Vi.

Her thoughts strayed again to Grandma Pearl's reason for keeping the scrapbook. Why hadn't she simply clipped the articles that interested her and stuffed them into a manila folder or an oversized envelope? Why go to all the trouble of cutting and pasting and organizing them? What aspect of that long-ago tragedy had captured her grandmother's attention to such an extent?

She found herself obsessed with those two names—Trula and Vi. She wondered how Melody's search in the old church records was coming along. Later that afternoon, Tracy decided it was time to pick Columbia's brain again. She cut some of the cooled fudge into bite-sized pieces and arranged them in a small cookie tin with a reindeer on the top.

"Sweets for the sweet," she quipped when Columbia opened her front door a short while later.

"Oh, how nice," Columbia greeted her, gratefully accepting the tin of fudge. "I've been hoping you'd stop by to tell me how you're getting along with the Woman in White mystery. Making any progress? I hope you won't be sorry down the road." She gave a slight shake of her head.

"Wait until you hear what I've found," Tracy told her, eager to share what she'd discovered so far. Noticing that the television was on, she asked, "Am I interrupting something?"

"It's my favorite Christmas movie. *Miracle on 34th Street* with Maureen O'Hara and little Natalie Wood. The original version." Columbia settled herself on the couch. "And that handsome John Payne. He was quite the heartthrob in his day."

"I can come back later," Tracy offered.

"No, young lady, you sit right down and tell me everything." Columbia used the remote control to click off the television. "I'm on pins and needles."

After declining the offer of coffee, hot chocolate, and zingy Russian tea, Tracy launched into her report. "I went to visit Elaine McLaren in the nursing home. She happens to be Poppy Maldonado's grandmother. Do you know her? She worked at Fancy Floral for decades."

Columbia nodded. "I'm acquainted with her. Elaine ran that florist shop for years. Is that why you went to see her? To ask about the white roses?"

"Yes," Tracy said. "But she wasn't willing to tell me what she knows. She insinuated that there are those who could be hurt by my prying."

Columbia's eyebrows arched high on her forehead. "My, sounds like she knows a thing or two."

"I'm certain she does." Tracy went on to tell her about the suitcase and its contents. Columbia listened, spellbound. She was particularly astonished to learn of the discovery of the old letter.

"It's hard to believe the police didn't find the letter all those years ago," Columbia declared. "And frankly, I'm surprised that Pearl didn't either." She shook her head in disbelief. "That's amazing. Nowadays, the police look for every bit of DNA evidence they can find—a single strand of hair, a fingernail, saliva on a toothbrush.

Anything. They didn't know about DNA back then, so perhaps they weren't as careful as they could have been and never thought to look under the lining."

"Remember too, the evidence was not related to a crime," Tracy pointed out. "The unnamed woman wasn't even listed as a missing person, because no one called the police to report her missing."

"True."

"I promised I wouldn't bother Elaine McLaren any further," Tracy went on, "but now that I've read the letter, I want to ask her if she once knew anyone named Trula or Vi. However, I can't keep hounding the woman. I know that."

Columbia considered this in silence for a moment before saying, "Maybe you could ask Poppy to let her grandmother know that you've located the suitcase and a letter and ask if she would be willing to talk about the contents with you. This new information might prompt her to reach out to you. If she doesn't, then keep your promise and don't press her any further."

"That's a good idea. I can even thank her again for talking with me before." Tracy sighed. "I think she might be hesitant to speak with me because she assumes I'm going to write about the incident for the newspaper. I told her this was a personal quest on Grandma Pearl's behalf, but I don't think she really believed me."

"Could be," Columbia acknowledged.

"Did I mention that she admitted to once seeing a picture of the mystery woman in a wedding photograph? She commented on how the police sketch was a good likeness."

Columbia leaned forward. "Now that's interesting. A wedding photo, you say?"

186

The Cameo Clue

"Framed," Tracy threw in.

"Did Elaine say she'd seen that particular photo here in Canton?"

"No, but I assumed so." Tracy then hastened to add, "Just because she once saw a photo of the Woman in White doesn't mean she necessarily knows who she is—or was. She might not even know anyone named Vi or Trula. I won't know until I ask her—if I ask her."

Columbia placed her fingers on her temples. "If one thinks about this too much it brings on a headache. The more you discover, Tracy, the more complicated it gets."

Tracy knew just what she meant. There were too many missing puzzle pieces, too many knots yet to untangle.

"Besides bringing you the fudge, I came over to ask if you knew of anyone named Trula or Vi who might have something to do with this mystery. Melody Bailey is checking the old membership lists at Faith Church. If she doesn't turn up any possibilities, then we're going to contact other churches in town."

"What makes you think either Trula or Aunt Vi went to church?"

"I don't know for sure. It's just a place to start," Tracy said. "I'm going to check the census records too. But without surnames, that'll take a lot of time. So, dear friend, do you—or have you—ever known anyone here in Canton named Vi-something?"

Columbia nodded. "Yes, my mother had a good friend named Vi—or that's what everyone called her. Her name was Oliva Dobbs. A spinster schoolteacher back in the day. They don't have spinsters anymore, do they? Vi Dobbs has long since passed away, and I couldn't tell you whether she was anyone's auntie or not."

Tracy bit her lip and frowned.

Vi Dobbs.

Olivia.

She'd assumed they needed to be searching for Vivians or Violets or Virginias—not women named Olivia. Tracy guessed she'd now have to cast a wider net in search of the unknown Aunt Vi.

Chapter Twenty-One

As soon as services were over on Sunday, Tracy dashed home to make sure everything was ready for the weekly family meal. She'd made a huge pot of ham and bean soup. Enticed by all the mouthwatering smells, Sadie remained constantly underfoot, following Tracy from the kitchen to the dining room and back to the kitchen again. As she stacked bowls and plates and paper cups on the end of the counter, Tracy felt relieved that they'd decided not to hold a party celebrating Grandma Pearl's birthday like they had last year. With the arrival of the new grandbaby in October and Amy's approaching wedding in January, there was simply too much to do.

She'd mentioned to Aunt Ruth last night on the phone that she still wanted to honor Grandma Pearl in some way after Christmas but just didn't have the time or energy to throw another party. Her aunt replied, "Solving the mystery of the Woman in White would have pleased your grandmother so much."

Aunt Ruth was right. That would be perfect. But was it possible?

The house was soon abuzz with bustle and noise as family members began to arrive. Aunt Ruth and Uncle Marvin got there first, bringing a large pan of cornbread and honey butter. Sara and Kevin arrived with Aiden and Zoe, who were so bundled up in coats, hats, and mittens that they appeared to be twice their normal size. Sadie

SECRETS FROM GRANDMA'S ATTIC

practically knocked the youngsters over in her excitement to welcome them.

Robin came in with Terry and Kai in tow. They brought a cheese and veggie tray arranged to look like a Christmas wreath. Last, but not least, Amy shuffled in with Jana and Matt tagging along behind carrying more food for the feast. When Jana skipped over to give her a big hug, Tracy glowed inside. It did her heart good too to see the broad smile on her face—no sulking, no pouting. Jana was her usual, beaming self. Tracy asked her to haul out the basket of colored blocks for the little ones to play with.

"Where's Miles?" Tracy asked. "Isn't he coming with Natalie and Colton?"

"They aren't coming today," Amy said lightly. When Tracy cast her a concerned glance, Amy laughed and shook her head. "Don't go worrying about anything, Sis. Nothing's wrong." She lowered her voice to add, "After our conversation about Jana and how she felt, I spoke with Miles about the kids and how they might be feeling now that the wedding is only weeks away—his kids and mine."

"What did he say?" Tracy probed.

"He agreed the transition may not be as easy as we thought. Even though the kids encouraged us to date in the first place, I was worried all along about neglecting Jana and Matt. I worried about how they might feel. Anyway, Miles took Natalie and Colton Christmas shopping. And then he's taking them out for hot fudge sundaes and a heart-to-heart talk about all of us living together in one house and becoming a family."

"But you're not postponing the wedding or anything, are you? Tracy asked hesitantly.

"Absolutely not," Amy assured her. "We just want to make sure we're not overlooking anyone's feelings and fears about the changes we'll all soon be facing."

Aunt Ruth called out from the other room, "Aren't Chad and Anna coming? I want to cuddle that new baby. I've already claimed the rocking chair for the afternoon."

Tracy laughed. "Not today," she called back. "Anna's sorority is hosting their annual family Christmas tea. She took Chad and the kids to that event. I think she was eager to show off the baby."

"Can't say I blame her one bit," Aunt Ruth declared. "I'll chase down Zoe and Aiden and get cuddles from them."

After gathering everyone around the table, Jeff said grace, and the eating and chatting began in earnest. Halfway through the meal, the doorbell rang. Sadie barked, and Kai sprang out of his chair, offering to answer the door. He returned to the dining room with Melody Bailey trailing behind him.

"I'm so sorry to interrupt your meal," she apologized. "But I wanted to give you this list, Tracy."

Tracy rose from the table. She assured Melody, "It's not a problem at all. Would you care to join us? There's plenty of food."

Everyone echoed the invitation, encouraging Melody to draw up a chair and have a bite to eat.

"No, really, I can't stay," Melody replied. "Lincoln and I have errands to run in Hannibal this afternoon." Turning to Tracy, she asked, "Do you have a minute?"

"Sure, let's go into the living room." Tracy led the way and offered Melody a seat.

Reaching into her oversized purse, Melody retrieved a list of names, which she handed to Tracy. "I checked every name in the church records looking for Vi this or Vi that. There was nothing for Trula, which didn't surprise me. I suspect that the young woman didn't live in Missouri at all—that's why your grandmother never turned up a hospital patient by that name. And, surprisingly, there weren't all that many women who might go by the name Vi either. I came up with a couple of Virginia's, but I'm guessing they went by Ginny or something similar and not Vi. That's what Maureen suggested anyway."

Tracy glanced over the list. Looking at the names, dates of membership, and local addresses, she wasn't certain any of them would be the woman they were searching for. Many of those who were members back in the 1940s and '50s would surely be deceased by now. Tracy supposed she could start calling on Monday morning to see what she could turn up.

"Thanks, Melody. You went to a lot of trouble, but I appreciate it."

"I'm afraid my search was not as fruitful as I thought it would be," Melody said sadly. "The church records don't tell us how old the women were at the time they became members. This really is not an efficient way to identify the elusive Aunt Vi after all."

Amy and Robin came in then, looking both curious and hopeful. "Are we intruding?" Amy asked. "We guessed Melody might be here about the Woman in White. I'm eager to hear what she has to share."

"Besides that, we're just plain nosy," Robin quipped.

Tracy shrugged. "I think our idea about searching church records wasn't so brilliant after all. Melody spent a lot of time going through the old lists at Faith Church, hoping to discover if Aunt Vi was possibly a member there."

Melody added, "I think Lincoln is right. We need to check census records."

Tracy added, "Yesterday when I spoke with Columbia, I realized we may have to expand our search."

"What do you mean?" Amy asked.

"We've been looking for women with names like Vivian or Viola and even Virginia," she said, "but Columbia told me her mother had a friend who taught school here in Canton years ago. Her name was Vi Dobbs, but her real name was Olivia."

Melody's dark eyes widened. "I hadn't thought of Olivia as a possible name to look for."

"Me neither," Tracy said.

"Maybe Aunt Vi's real name was Olive," Robin put in. "That's an old-fashioned name you may have to consider too."

"Without surnames, perusing the census records won't be a cakewalk either," Amy pointed out.

Tracy's shoulders slumped. "I know. But we've got to keep looking."

"I hope you don't think it was presumptuous of me, but I told Maureen not to worry about contacting other churches about their membership lists until after the holidays," Melody said. "Christmas is always a hectic time for a church secretary. And besides, her husband isn't well, and Maureen has her hands full with family obligations."

Maureen's husband was battling cancer. Tracy didn't want to burden the woman with what might prove to be a wild-goose chase. "Before we contact other churches, I think we should tackle the census records," she said.

SECRETS FROM GRANDMA'S ATTIC

Robin reached for the list and gave it a quick glance. "You might want to consider looking at the property tax list for 1944 too. If Aunt Vi was a homeowner here, her name might show up. I'd be happy to help with that, but not until the holidays are over. This is my busiest time of year at the shop."

"Thanks," Tracy said. She appreciated her cousin's willingness to help.

"This may sound rather corny, but what about placing an ad in the *Times*?" Amy suggested. "Something along the lines of 'Seeking local relatives of Aunt Vi with niece Trula. Have family heirlooms that belong to you. Please contact Tracy Doyle at the *Lewis Country Times*.'"

Melody and Tracy exchanged a glance. Robin straightened as she passed the list back to Tracy. "I think that's a great idea!"

"I'm not so sure," Melody said. "You might get all sorts of women coming out of the woodwork, hoping to take possession of something valuable."

They all shifted their attention to Amy, who grinned and shrugged. "Hey, it works in novels and the movies all the time."

The women shared a laugh.

Jeff moseyed in then, clutching a carrot stick in one hand. "What's so funny?"

"My little sister," Tracy said, giving Amy's arm a squeeze.

"The natives are growing restless for dessert," he said. "Can I bring out those peppermint pies?"

Tracy nodded. "Sure thing."

"I'll go put on some coffee," Robin volunteered. She followed Jeff out of the room.

The Cameo Clue

"You sure you won't stay for pie and coffee?" Tracy asked Melody.

Melody shook her head. "No, like I said, Lincoln and I have plans. I just wanted you to have this list in case you want to continue with your investigation. I can't guarantee anything positive will come of it. But who knows? One of the younger women on the list may have been named for their great-aunt Vi—the very woman we're looking for."

Tracy felt a spark of hope. "You know, that's possible."

"I still think advertising would be quicker," Amy spoke up. "Even if Aunt Vi who wrote the letter has long since passed away, she may have a family member who recognizes the two names and is eager to claim a family heirloom."

Tracy silently agreed. It would be easy enough to place an ad in the newspaper. Being an employee, she could probably do so for free, or at least at a discounted rate. However, recalling what Columbia had said about the couple who long ago had fraudulently claimed the young woman in the cemetery as their daughter in hopes of taking possession of her belongings, Tracy wasn't sure she wanted to deal with that sort of thing.

"I'll think about it," she said. And she would, really.

But even if she decided to place an ad as Amy suggested, it would have to wait until after Christmas.

SECRETS FROM GRANDMA'S ATTIC

November 19, 1944
Oaklawn Retreat

Dear Aunt Vi,

Guess what? More good news! I was allowed to join the others in the dining room last night. It was so thrilling I could hardly eat. But rest assured, the hovering nurses made sure I did. When they told me I could get dressed and go downstairs for dinner, I delightedly exclaimed, "Egads and little fishes!" That made them all laugh.

I was positively giddy by the opportunity. I could feel my cheeks flush with the joy of it. Nurse Booth cautioned me about getting overexcited. That sort of thing can raise one's body temperature, you know, and then it's back to enforced bed rest. She advised me to remain calm. I did try. But it was so exciting to eat at the long dining room table with other patients. I felt like a human being again, not a log. There was pork roast and sweet potatoes. Delicious! We had baked apples with warm custard sauce for dessert.

I think I'm getting rather chubby. I mentioned it to the doctor and asked if maybe I should be exercising a little. Dr. Spooner said yes. Every morning I'm to walk downstairs to get weighed. Funny man! That's not exactly what I meant. But I am allowed to walk the grounds now—not too far and

The Cameo Clue

not too long. Jilly finally visited and brought me my winter clothes and my pretty wool coat that was new when I married Tom. So I can wear regular clothes now. Having Jilly here was the best thing ever! She brought heaps of cards and notes from the other girls at Mrs. Batterson's boardinghouse. And a tin of homemade fudge. I shared with the other women in the ward, and it was like a holiday celebration. Everyone loved Jilly too.

I still must rest in bed for four hours a day. There's also the enforced sitting outside period. No matter that it's quite cold now. They bundle us up in blankets and arrange us on the sunny porch to breathe all that healing fresh air. I suppose it must be working. I am getting better after all.

There's a patient here who just came back from overseas—a veteran. He lost an eye to a piece of German shrapnel over in Europe in one of those countries I can't identify on a map if my life depended on it. He wears a black eye patch, like a pirate. Poor guy. It's bad enough getting wounded in action, but then to come home and discover you're sick with tuberculosis too. What bad luck!

A counselor came through today to speak with me about the future. She wanted to know what I plan to do when I am allowed to go home. I didn't tell her I don't have a home to go to. I was afraid that would delay any hope for a release before Christmas. I did tell her I'd like a job when I get out, that I need to return to work. She said she might be able to help with that but advised me against taking a job in a textile factory or in a corn processing plant. They have one here in Jacksonville right outside of town. Too much dust in the air, she said, and that's bad for my lungs.

Someone donated a player piano to the sanatorium along with a box full of music rolls. Now we have music while we eat in the dining room. And there are bridge parties sometimes afterwards—but I don't know how to play. I was finally allowed to explore the library and the sewing room too. There are women here making their own clothes. I don't sew. I mean, I can repair a loose hem and sew on a button, but I don't know how to make a dress or anything.

Do you sew, Aunt Vi?

Mona's mother brought her a portable Crosley companion radio that she keeps on her bedside table. We can now listen to Perry Como and Bing Crosby and Vaughn Monroe while we get our mandatory bed rest. But we're not allowed to listen to war news or any other news broadcasts. Might make us agitated, the nurse said.

The woman in the bed across the room from me is new. Her name is Tamar, like in the Bible. She's quiet and shy. She seems kind of scared about being here. So does her husband. He came to visit on Sunday—a kind little man with sad eyes. He brought her a Whitman's Sampler full of scrumptious chocolates. Tamara has no appetite at all, so she passed the *box around for us to share. I helped myself. Who doesn't like chocolates?*

Please write, Aunt Vi. Or have Dory write if you're too busy. I haven't heard from you in ever so long. I think maybe you're sick with influenza or pneumonia or something. Pneumonia can be dangerous. The nurses tell us that all the time. TB patients are susceptible to it, I've been told.

I pray for you. And Dory and Uncle Alfred too. You're the only family I have left in all the world. Do remember that, won't you?

Sincerely,

Trula

P.S. We are going to have a Thanksgiving feast here with turkey and cranberries and everything. I'm so glad the sanatorium doesn't have to eat on rations!

P.P.S. Jilly and Mrs. B and the girls at the boarding-house took up a collection and sent me some money to buy myself something I've been dying to have. Wasn't that the sweetest thing? There's enough to buy a train ticket and a bus ticket too. I could come see you at Christmas, and it wouldn't cost you a thing! Hint, hint.

Chapter Twenty-Two

On Monday morning, Tracy whipped up some cheesy scrambled eggs and coffee for breakfast and then dressed in a slim corduroy skirt and a pink blouse with ruffles at the throat and wrists. As she regarded herself in the full-length mirror on the back of her bedroom door, she realized how attractive the old cameo brooch would look with her outfit. Did she dare wear it? It seemed a pity to keep it hidden away in her dresser drawer.

"Why not?" she said aloud. Retrieving it from her dresser, she pinned it on, making sure the clasp was firmly closed. Despite the tarnish, the brooch was pretty and added a vintage touch to her outfit. If anyone commented on the brooch, she'd come right out and tell them it had once belonged to the mysterious Woman in White. That would be a real conversation starter for sure.

Tracy wondered if anyone would even notice the brooch. Most people didn't have a keen eye for vintage jewelry. In a strange way, wearing it made her feel close to both Trula and Grandma Pearl. She felt too that it was a celebratory gesture. Against all odds, the old suitcase had been located along with a letter. Now she had two names—Trula and Aunt Vi. She suppressed a nagging thought that the aunt who'd signed the letter might not have lived in Canton at all. That she had lived somewhere else and had discouraged Trula from coming for a Christmas visit. Thus discouraged, Trula came to Canton instead. But if so, who had she come to visit? And if Aunt Vi hadn't lived in Canton, where had she lived?

As soon as he'd eaten, Jeff dashed off to the college. Tracy filled Sadie's dishes with dog food and fresh water, answered a few emails on her laptop, and then made her way to the office, bundled to the teeth. It was definitely getting colder. Could snow be on the way?

At the office, she learned that Eric had called an impromptu meeting of the staff. Tracy quickly shrugged off her coat, retrieved a yellow pad from her desk, and made her way to the conference room, taking a chair next to Annette. Her friend, of course, noticed the brooch and tilted her head to one side questioningly.

"Is that…?"

"It is," Tracy said.

But Annette's reaction was nothing compared to Eric's. When he saw it, he startled. He gave Tracy an odd, questioning frown, glanced at the brooch again, and then called the meeting to order in a rather distracted way. Tracy had no doubt he'd recognized the cameo. After all, Trula was wearing it on her coat in the police sketch.

Tracy wondered, if by wearing it today, she would provoke Eric's anger. She hoped not. He didn't appear to be angry. He took care of the business at hand, doling out a few assignments and requesting possible ideas for soliciting new advertisers for the next issue. They were done in less than two hours, at which time he thanked everyone for their time and dismissed them.

"If you could stay for a minute, Tracy," he added in a mild tone, "I'd like to speak with you."

SECRETS FROM GRANDMA'S ATTIC

Tracy felt her stomach lurch. Wearing the pin had been foolish after all. Would he see the gesture as her flaunting her interest in the mysterious woman after he'd made it clear he didn't want her pursuing the topic at the office?

Annette gave her a sympathetic pat on the shoulder in passing. Jake raised his eyebrows. With a heavy heart, Tracy lowered herself back into her seat. She had so hoped this week would start off in a more satisfactory way without any tantrums or confrontations.

Eric followed the others to the door and then closed it behind them. He returned to his place at the long table and sat down. He scooted the rolling chair up close so he could rest his elbows on the table. Lacing his fingers together, he gave Tracy a sheepish smile. "I owe you an apology, Tracy."

Tracy felt a twinge of astonishment. Now here was a pleasant change. She remained silent, wondering what he intended to apologize for.

"I've been a real jerk lately—to the entire staff, but to you especially," Eric went on.

Wondering if this was where she was supposed to say something soothing and self-deprecating, Tracy decided not to say a word. What Eric said was true. He had been a jerk. His behavior had been atrocious.

"I've been dealing with some family issues," he went on, "but those reasons don't excuse my attitude of late. I really am sorry."

Tracy said, "Apology accepted." And she meant it. On the other hand, she wanted to make her escape before he mentioned the cameo or began criticizing her work. What was that old saying? Get out while the getting is good? "Are we through? May I go now?"

202

The Cameo Clue

"Not yet. I need to speak with you about...about something rather personal."

"Is it about my work?" Tracy held her breath. It would be awful to be fired right before Christmas. Being fired at any time was depressing enough, but right before Christmas was even worse.

"No, your work is fine," Eric hastened to assure her. He ran a hand through his dark hair, making it poke up here and there in a windblown way. "I don't even know where to start."

Tracy bit back the sarcastic response about starting at the beginning. She didn't want to appear disrespectful. Not after he'd gone to so much trouble to apologize.

"Elaine McLaren called me this morning before you arrived," Eric said.

Tracy sat up a little straighter. She'd hardly expected this. Was Elaine suddenly willing to talk? "Oh, did she leave a message for me? I visited her at the nursing home last week—as you know. I gave her my number here." Tracy didn't mention that she'd gone to see Elaine twice.

"No, she actually wanted to speak to me about your conversation with her last week," Eric went on. "Elaine said you told her that you have a certain cameo brooch in your possession. She wanted me to find out if that was true. I'm guessing that might be it." He made a gesture toward the cameo at her throat.

Her fingers fluttering to the old-fashioned pin, Tracy said, "Yes, it is."

"It doesn't belong to you, I know. Can you tell me how you came to have it?" His voice remained calm, his expression more puzzled than angry.

SECRETS FROM GRANDMA'S ATTIC

For a moment, Tracy became lost in thought, wondering why Elaine would call her boss and not her. Didn't Elaine trust her? Was it possible that Elaine and Eric were friends or acquaintances? If so, Poppy hadn't mentioned it. Perhaps she hadn't thought to do so. And did it matter anyway?

"The cameo," Eric prompted.

Tracy cleared her throat. "Do you remember last week I showed you the scrapbook my grandmother kept regarding the Woman in White?" When Eric nodded, Tracy said, "It was pinned to one of the pages."

"But that doesn't explain how come your grandmother had it," Eric said.

Tracy shrugged. "I can't be sure, of course, but my pastor suggested that she volunteered to keep it safe, hoping one day to be able to identify the woman when and if someone recognized the brooch as a family heirloom. Apparently, the authorities agreed, and that's why the woman wasn't buried with it. They hoped someone would identify her from the police sketch or perhaps recognize the brooch."

Eric nodded. For a moment, he leaned back in his chair, silent and lost in thought.

"But I don't understand why Elaine McLaren called you about the cameo," Tracy said. Again, she touched the pin. "I would have been more than willing to return to the nursing home to show it to her. I don't know why she didn't feel she could speak to me about it. I urged her to call me."

Ignoring her question, Eric said, "Tell me more about your grandmother's interest in the Woman in White."

Tracy sat up a little straighter, pleased that Eric was suddenly interested. She summarized what she'd told him before and then

The Cameo Clue

went on to explain about her grandmother's letter writing campaign, how she reached out to area hospitals, hoping one of them would recognize the young woman as a recent patient. Eric asked several pertinent questions and listened to her answers with keen interest.

At the end of Tracy's detailed recital, he said, "Your grandmother went to a lot of trouble for a stranger." There was a hint of admiration in his tone.

"Grandma Pearl was special," Tracy said wistfully. "She treated others that way too." With a short sigh, she added, "It concerned my grandmother to the point that she started the scrapbook and tried as hard as she could to learn the identity of the mysterious young woman. I couldn't help feeling that I should take up the task where my grandmother left off." After a moment's pause, Tracy added, "As of late last week, I have the woman's suitcase in my possession too. And her purse."

That caught Eric's immediate attention. His eyebrows arched high. He leaned forward. "What? How is that possible after all these years? Where in the world did you dig that up?"

Tracy couldn't help smiling. "Danica Jones at the county building discovered it in an old storage closet. Lincoln Bailey gave the suitcase to me. He and I examined the contents together, along with his wife Melody."

With a shake of his head, Eric said, "It's almost too hard to believe. Did you find anything that might help you give a name to the Woman in White?"

"We did," Tracy said. "There was nothing at all to identify her in the purse, not even a ration card, but we discovered a letter—handwritten, on a single sheet of stationery. It was addressed to someone named Trula

SECRETS FROM GRANDMA'S ATTIC

and signed by someone named Aunt Vi. That's not much to go on, I'll admit, but it's more than we had before, and I'm not giving up."

Eric swallowed hard. He picked up a pencil and idly tapped the table with it. "I don't believe this. It can't be a coincidence." Taking a deep breath, he asked, "What about the envelope? Any last names? Addresses?"

Tracy shook her head. "No envelope. Lincoln suggested that first names weren't much of a lead at all." Then, with a self-conscious laugh, she added, "Despite his skepticism, I told him that one day I'd return the suitcase and the cameo to the woman's family."

Eric gave her a penetrating stare. He dropped the pencil. After a rather awkward pause, he said, "Tracy, you may find this hard to believe, but I may be able to help you do just that."

Chapter Twenty-Three

Tracy didn't try to hide her surprise. Tilting her head, she asked, "What do you mean?"

"It's a long story, and I don't even know the half of it," Eric said. "I want you to come to Brookdale with me."

"To visit Elaine McLaren again?" It still didn't make sense to Tracy why the elderly woman had contacted Eric about the cameo rather than calling her as Tracy had encouraged her to do.

Eric sighed. "Actually, I think you should meet my grandmother." He gave her a sad smile.

"Does she live at Brookdale too?" If so, that would explain why they'd run into each other last week at the front door when she and Poppy were leaving and Eric was just arriving.

He nodded. "I want her to see that." He pointed to the cameo pinned to her blouse. "And it might be a good thing if you could bring the suitcase along too."

"All right," Tracy agreed. "But do you mind if I ask why? You've certainly roused my curiosity."

Again, Eric ran a hand through his dark hair. "My mother has Parkinson's. You may or may not know that. Anyway, it's one of the reasons I took this job and moved to Canton. When she began to lose her balance and have frequent falls, my sisters and I knew Mom

SECRETS FROM GRANDMA'S ATTIC

could no longer care for her mother. We decided it was best to move Granny into the nursing home where she could have round-the-clock professional care."

Tracy sighed. "That's a hard decision to make. I'm sorry."

Eric pursed his lips. "Anyway, it's become clear that Granny will never be able to live alone again. We've decided to put her house up for sale. Before we can do that, however, we need to go through her belongings and decide what to keep, give away, or sell. It's proving to be quite a chore." He heaved a sigh. "To make a long story short, we recently found a black-and-white photograph of a young woman who is a dead ringer for the lady known as the Woman in White. She's even wearing that brooch in the photo." He lifted his chin to indicate the cameo on Tracy's blouse.

For a moment, Tracy found herself speechless with excitement. Her heart began to pound against her ribs. A thousand unanswered questions buzzed around in her head like flies on honey. Was it possible that the photograph Eric referred to was the same one Elaine had mentioned seeing years ago? She had to find out.

"By any chance is it a framed wedding photograph?" She held her breath waiting for his response.

"It could be." Eric drew a deep breath and sighed. "The young woman isn't wearing a typical wedding dress though. She has on a two-piece suit with a corsage pinned near her shoulder. The young man is in a military uniform. 'July 1943' is written in pencil on the back."

"Are there names written on the back too?" Tracy asked, her pulse throbbing at her temples.

Eric nodded. The wrinkles between his eyes grew deeper.

208

"Is Trula the name of the bride?" Her throat was so dry Tracy could barely swallow.

"Yes. Tom and Trula Drybeck." He frowned. "But how do you know about the photograph? You can't possibly have seen it before."

Tracy shook her head. "I haven't, but Elaine McLaren has. She told me so, but she didn't tell me where or when. She didn't tell me who owned the photograph either."

"Now that's interesting. Very interesting." Eric stroked his chin. For a moment, he seemed to be lost in thought. "I think you and I should talk with my grandmother—and maybe with Elaine too. Let's show them the cameo and the contents of the suitcase. I want to see how they react. Granny has her good days and her bad days. Her memory isn't what it used to be."

Tracy's heart went out to him. "It's not easy watching someone you love fade away."

"That's the painful truth," Eric agreed.

"Did you show her the photograph after you recognized the similarity to the Woman in White?"

"Granny didn't appear to recognize either the man or the woman," he explained.

"Even when you told her the names on the back?" Tracy pressed.

"The names did ring a bell. Lately, she's been fretful, saying odd things about needing to remember flowers for Trula's grave. She must know something about the couple—or at least the woman in the photograph. She mentioned the name Trula, but didn't seem to connect it to the woman in the photograph."

Tracy took a deep breath. Trula's grave!

SECRETS FROM GRANDMA'S ATTIC

"I'm somewhat concerned about the whole thing," Eric replied. "I don't want to cause my grandmother any trouble or undue stress."

"What kind of trouble?" Tracy asked.

"I don't know exactly," he said. "After Granny mentioned Trula's grave a couple of times, I looked up the cemetery records to see if anyone named Trula is buried there. I couldn't find anyone by that name. Then in my research on another subject, I came across a brief mention of the Woman in White. I went to Tawny Hagstrom at the historical society for more information. Then you showed me your grandmother's scrapbook. The resemblance between the young woman in the police sketch and the woman in the old photograph at Granny's house was just too uncanny. That's when I started thinking they were the same woman."

"And now that we know the name of the Woman in White, we know for sure that it's the same woman," Tracy said. "We just need Elaine and your grandmother—if she can—to help fill in the blanks. Is Elaine a friend of your grandmother's? They're about the same age."

"Yes, Elaine and Granny have been friends since they were in fourth or fifth grade," Eric told her.

"Then you must know that Elaine worked at the floral shop for decades. That's why I went to visit her the other day. She knows something about the white roses placed on the grave, but she wouldn't tell me what she knows. She said it wasn't her secret to share."

Eric's eyes widened. "She said that?" He leaned back in the chair. "This becomes more intriguing by the minute. My sisters and I have been wondering if Granny knows something about that long-ago incident. She might know something that was possibly illegal or immoral. You can see why we're concerned."

The Cameo Clue

"But your grandmother would have been a child in 1944. She couldn't possibly be involved," Tracy hastened to assure him.

"That's true," Eric agreed, "but it doesn't mean she doesn't know something that needs to come out in the open. I don't understand her references to the roses for the grave. You're right, she would have been a child when the woman died. And yet someone placed roses on the grave for years. Tawny Hagstrom filled me in on some of the history and how no one has ever claimed to be the one who placed the roses there. No one has ever been caught in the act either."

"That's true," Tracy said. "It was all very clandestine. For a while, I thought my grandmother may have been the person who placed the flowers there—simply as a kind gesture. Then I considered the doctor who tried to save the young woman's life. I also toyed with the idea that someone on the benevolence committee may have felt obligated to buy flowers for the grave, but nothing explains the decades of secrecy. There's nothing to be ashamed of in remembering the woman with a floral bouquet on the anniversary of her death, and yet the gesture has been a secret since Day One."

"Very mysterious," Eric observed. "My grandmother knows something about it, and I need to find out what that is. And I need to find out while there's still time. Granny will soon be ninety years old. Her health is poor. I don't want her to carry this secret to her grave."

Tracy agreed. She too was determined to get to the bottom of it. "I think you're right, that we should talk with your grandmother and Elaine together. Considering your grandmother's health issues, I feel we might learn more from Elaine. If we question them together, Elaine might be willing to share what she knows. In fact, I think she holds the key to solving the mystery."

SECRETS FROM GRANDMA'S ATTIC

Eric pushed his chair back. "I suppose you could be right."

"I think I am," Tracy said. "But I can understand your reluctance to keep digging into this."

"You think I'm reluctant?" He gave Tracy a quizzical frown.

"I think you have mixed feelings. On the one hand you're afraid your grandmother might be implicated in something. Once a skeleton in the closet is exposed, it can't be ignored. On the other hand, your journalistic instincts drive you to pursue the truth. In my opinion, truth is always worth pursuing—no matter what the outcome."

"You're right, Tracy. Let's go see Granny." Eric rose.

Tracy did the same. "But there's one thing we haven't mentioned yet, and I'm curious. The letter I found in the suitcase—it was addressed to Trula and signed Aunt Vi. Do you have any idea who Aunt Vi might be?"

Eric placed his hand on his hips. "Absolutely. I'm pretty sure it's Violet Clark—my maternal great-grandmother, which would make Trula and my grandmother cousins."

Chapter Twenty-Four

Tracy agreed to meet Eric at Brookdale after first going home to pick up the suitcase. Once there, she let Sadie out for a quick romp in the backyard and decided to take the letter too in case Elaine or Eric's grandmother cared to see the contents. And of course she was wearing the cameo, which she thought would be what they would really want to see the most.

On her way there, Tracy made a quick stop at Fancy Floral, where she discovered Gwen Montgomery behind the counter.

"Hello again," Gwen greeted her. "Want to buy another poinsettia?"

"Actually, I'm wondering if you have any white roses and, if so, could you put half a dozen in a vase—tied up with a red velvet bow?"

Gwen arched an eyebrow. "I'm intrigued. Does this have something to do with the mysterious Woman in White that we discussed the other day?"

"Yes, I think it does," Tracy told her with a conspiratorial smile.

With deft fingers, Gwen selected six white roses from the large refrigerator. She carefully placed these in a slender glass vase with bits of green stuff that looked like ferns and sprigs of baby's breath and then tied a red ribbon around the vase. It was an attractive arrangement. The roses had a subtle, pleasant scent.

SECRETS FROM GRANDMA'S ATTIC

Tracy thanked her and paid with a credit card. She wanted to present the flower arrangement to Eric's grandmother. She thought perhaps the sight or scent of the flowers would trigger a memory or two.

Eric waited for her in the lobby—rather impatiently, hands thrust into the front pockets of his brown corduroys. "What took you so long?" he asked. His tone softened when he noticed the vase of flowers. "Are those for Granny?"

"Yes," Tracy said. "I've read that scent can sometimes trigger long-suppressed memories. Maybe seeing or smelling the roses will prompt her to recall something about putting roses on Trula's grave."

Eric nodded. "Elaine is waiting for us in Granny's room. My sister Ann is here too, by the way. She stopped by with a couple of clean sweaters for Granny, and when I told her that you were coming, she decided to stay. She's eager to see the cameo and the suitcase too."

She passed the suitcase to him.

Eric handled it carefully, shaking his head with disbelief. "Trula and Grandma Vi. Maybe we'll learn something at last."

Tracy followed him down the corridor to the opposite wing of the facility and to his grandmother's room. She was mindful of an excited eagerness. Her hands began to perspire inside her gloves, so she removed them, stashing them into the pocket of her coat. Tracy prayed this would be one of the elderly woman's good days. When they entered the room, she first noticed Elaine McLaren in her wheelchair. Tracy was hard-pressed to describe the expression on the older woman's face—part resentment and part anxiety. There was a touch of expectation there too. Even before Tracy shrugged out of her coat, Elaine noticed the cameo pinned to her blouse and raised her eyebrows with surprise.

"Tracy, this is my grandmother, Dorinda Watson, and my sister Ann." Eric introduced her to the others.

"Everyone calls our grandmother Dory," Ann explained. She was a short brunette in her late thirties with dark wavy hair and eyes like her brother's.

"Nice to meet you, Dory," Tracy said. "These are for you." She handed the slender vase to the elderly woman slumped in an armchair by the window. Her face was heavily lined, her gray hair chopped short. But there was something around the nose and mouth that resembled her grandson and granddaughter. Tracy could tell immediately that they were related.

Dory looked pleased with the flowers. "Thank you. Who are you again?"

"I'm Tracy Doyle. I work with Eric."

"Do you know my friend Elaine?" She reached out with a heavily veined hand to touch Elaine's sleeve. "She's my best friend."

Tracy smiled, first at Dory and then at Elaine. "Yes, we've met."

The small room was crowded. Ann stepped out into the corridor and returned with a folding chair for Tracy and then took a seat on the edge of her grandmother's bed. Eric remained standing. When Ann reached for the flower vase, Eric shook his head. Tracy supposed he remembered what she'd said about scent and sight bringing back memories. She hoped the flowers would do the trick.

Eric cleared his throat. "Elaine, thanks for coming. I have some things I want to share with you and Granny, and then I'm hoping you will share what you know as well. We're going to get to the bottom of this Woman in White mystery. I think it's time, don't you?" He faced Elaine directly.

SECRETS FROM GRANDMA'S ATTIC

"As I told Tracy, it's not my secret to tell." Elaine cast a meaningful glance in Dory's direction.

"Granny has been fretting about flowers for Trula's grave. We can't ease her anxiety about the matter if we don't know the details," Eric explained.

"It's time for the secret to come out," Ann added. "Tracy found the suitcase that Trula Drybeck brought with her when she came to Canton in 1944."

Eric picked up the tale. "Inside was a short letter written to her and signed 'Aunt Vi.' I feel certain that Aunt Vi is our great-grandmother—Violet Clark. Granny's mother. Now we want you and Granny to fill in the missing details."

"Vi?" Dory sat up straight. "Violet. That was my mother's name. But everyone called her Vi."

"That's right, Granny," Ann said encouragingly. "Your mother's name was Violet. And she had a niece named Trula—your cousin."

Dory frowned. "Are these flowers for Trula's grave?" She raised the vase and sniffed the petals.

"No, those are for you," Tracy told her. "Do we need to get flowers for Trula's grave too?"

"Yes, Mother said so. But it has to be a secret." Dory nodded knowingly. "We have to keep the secret."

"Why?" Eric pressed. He cast Tracy a poignant, sidelong glance. Then, in a gentle tone, he said, "Granny, you don't have to keep the secret anymore."

"I don't?" Dory fixed anxious eyes upon him. She looked helplessly at Elaine.

The Cameo Clue

Elaine turned, fixing her gaze on Eric. With a heavy sigh, she said, "I suppose I should explain."

"We wish you would," Tracy said.

"Is it safe?" Dory asked.

Eric smiled and touched her arm. "Yes, Granny, it's safe."

Dory blinked a few times before once again smelling the roses.

Elaine cleared her throat. "You've got to understand that Violet Clark—that's Dory's mother—was terrified that she'd done something wrong when she didn't immediately come forward to identify her niece after Trula died."

"She's the one who bought the flowers for the grave each year?" Tracy probed.

"Yes, Violet Clark."

"How do you know that?" Ann asked. "You were only a child when Trula died."

"I started working at the floral shop when I was a teenager," Elaine explained. "One of the clerks there told me about the special December order. The customer would pay in cash, and I was to keep quiet about it. She didn't know the woman personally, but that first Christmas when Mrs. Clark walked in to order white roses, I knew who she was. As Dory said, we were best friends growing up. Mrs. Clark swore me to secrecy too, and I promised not to tell."

"Did she ever say why it had to remain a secret?" Eric asked.

Elaine shrugged. "No, and I didn't ask. I was rather excited to be part of the mystery. At first I thought Mrs. Clark was just doing something nice and that she didn't want anyone to know and make a fuss about it. I'd read about the December bouquet in the newspaper.

SECRETS FROM GRANDMA'S ATTIC

It was fun to be in on the secret. It wasn't until much later that Dory explained to me that her mother was scared about the police discovering Trula's identity."

Tracy leaned forward. "Why was she scared of that?"

Dory spoke up. "Trula was sick. She wasn't supposed to come to our house. Mama didn't invite her." She turned her attention to Eric. "She wasn't supposed to come. We weren't expecting her. Mama wrote to her and told her not to come. Because of the TB." She plucked a single white rose from the vase and held it to her nose. Ann removed the vase and placed it on the dresser.

Elaine gave her friend a glance with such empathy that Tracy realized how close the two women must have been through the years.

"She wasn't supposed to come," Dory repeated.

"That's right," Eric chimed in. "We have Violet's letter telling Trula not to come. We have it right here." He carefully removed the old letter from the suitcase, unfolded it, and offered it to his grandmother.

Dory looked at it and appeared to read the short missive. Shaking her head, she said sadly, "Trula came anyway, and she died."

"But why didn't Grandma Vi identify her before they buried Trula in the cemetery?" Eric asked.

When Dory turned her head to stare at the wall, lost in thoughts of her own, Elaine took her friend's hand. "It's safe, Dory. We can talk about it now. We can tell them why your mother was afraid. She isn't in any trouble, and neither are you. It's okay to tell."

Dory took a shuddering breath. "Mama was afraid. The longer she stayed quiet, the more afraid she became. She feared she'd done something criminal by not letting anyone know about Trula. She was afraid people would think we encouraged my cousin to leave that place where she was staying, that her death was our fault. But Mama wrote and told her not to come."

Looking at Eric and Tracy, Elaine added, "It must all seem so silly to you now, but at the time tuberculosis was highly contagious, and there was a stigma attached to the disease. People were ashamed to admit they had family members with TB. Mrs. Clark was terrified that Trula would bring it here, that Dory would become infected with the disease or even Mr. Clark, who was already ill."

"Dad was sick," Dory said.

"Yes, he was," Elaine confirmed. "Mr. Clark had pneumonia that winter, and he also had a heart condition. Dory's mother was quite concerned about him. She didn't want Trula coming to add to her worries. She wrote to Trula, telling her so. Why Trula came anyway, no one knows."

"Homesick, perhaps?" Tracy proposed.

"But this wasn't her home," Dory said with surprising clarity. "She'd never come to see us before." Then, with an anxious note in her voice, she added, "She wasn't supposed to come at all."

Eric patted his grandmother's hand. "It's okay, Granny. It happened a long time ago. You don't need to worry about it anymore."

"Mama made me promise not to tell. I never told anyone— except Elaine." Her chin quivered. "I never told." She choked back a sob.

Ann gave her grandmother's shoulders a squeeze. "Everything is okay now. No one is in any trouble."

Elaine added, "I kept the promise I made to Mrs. Clark for years. I never told a soul that she bought flowers once a year for the grave of the mysterious woman. It wasn't until many years later that I happened to notice Trula's photograph on a bookshelf." She turned to Tracy. "The one I told you about—the one I'd seen. I'd borrowed a book from Dory and discovered the photo when I put the book back on the shelf."

"Trula Drybeck's wedding photograph in the frame," Tracy prompted.

"Yes, that's the one," Elaine affirmed. "Only then did I suspect that the mysterious woman she was buying flowers for might be a member of their family. I asked Dory about it. She told me the woman in the photo was her cousin. When I pointed out that the woman in the photograph and the woman in the sketch were the same, Dory explained everything to me. She made me promise not to tell, because she and her mother might get in trouble with the police. Mr. Clark had passed away by that time. They lived in fear of having broken a law of some kind."

"Elaine promised not to tell," Dory spoke up.

"And I never did," Elaine said, patting her arm again.

"Mama was afraid we'd have to pay for Trula's funeral, so she didn't tell anyone we knew Trula. Then after my cousin was buried, Mama was afraid we'd go to jail for not coming forward when the police asked for help in identifying her. Mama was so afraid for years." Dory sighed heavily and twirled the rose between her thin fingers. "She told me I would probably go to jail too, for hindering a police investigation. I was just a girl. I believed her. I was afraid too."

Eric's eyes rounded. "Granny, I'm so sorry you've had to live with this for so long. I didn't know. But I assure you, there's no reason to be afraid any longer."

The Cameo Clue

"Dory, when your mother passed away, you took over the task of ordering the flowers for the grave, right?" Tracy asked.

Dory nodded. "Yes, Mama wanted me to. We had to be careful at first so no one would catch us doing it. After a while, people forgot all about Trula, and it was easier. We could go anytime. As long as we saw no one else walking or driving in the cemetery, we would leave the bouquet on the grave."

Tracy turned to Elaine. "When I spoke with Gwen Montgomery at Fancy Floral last week, she said it's been years since anyone has placed an order for the flowers for the grave."

Elaine shrugged. In a quiet tone, she replied, "I've not worked there for years, and Dory seemed to have forgotten, so I thought it best to let the tradition cease. Besides, how was Dory to get the flowers to the cemetery? She's not been well, and really, there was no reason for this to go on any longer."

"I agree," Eric declared warmly. "There's been enough fear and guilt and shame."

Tracy unpinned the cameo from her blouse and placed it in Dory's hand. "Dory, this belongs to you now. Trula wore it on her wedding day. I'm sure it must be a family heirloom. She would want you to have it."

Dory looked at the pin. "Grandma Herman," she said reminiscently. "I remember this brooch."

"My great-great-grandmother," Eric added for Tracy's benefit.

"It's yours now," Tracy said again.

Smiling, Dory held it out for Elaine to admire. "It's pretty, isn't it?"

"Yes, it's very pretty," Elaine said, smiling too.

"Have you seen Trula's headstone? It's very nice, don't you think so?" Dory asked of no one in particular.

"Dory, my grandmother was one of those on the committee that ordered the stone," Tracy told her.

"How kind. What was your grandmother's name?"

"Pearl Wallace Allen," Tracy told her.

When Dory shrugged, Tracy supposed that the elderly woman hadn't known or didn't remember Grandma Pearl.

"Would you like to see Trula's wedding picture?" Dory asked, looking at them all in turn. "She was a pretty bride. She wore this brooch on her wedding day."

"I would like that very much," Tracy said.

Eric piped in, "Me too."

"Maybe you'd like to read her letters too," Dory added. "Mama saved them all."

Chapter Twenty-Five

Two days later Eric arrived at the newspaper office beaming with good humor. He carried a shoebox under one arm and a large container of assorted pastries from Buttermilk Bakeshop in his other hand. "Goodies in the break room," he called out by way of greeting to the astonished staff. "And Merry Christmas!"

Tracy, Annette, and everyone else stared at him with round eyes before Tracy hastened to echo, "Merry Christmas." Edmund and Jake got up from their desks to follow Eric to the break room, hoping to get first pick of the pastries. When he exited the break room, Eric pulled Tracy aside, saying, "I brought Trula's letters. I thought you'd like to see them. The ones she wrote to my great-grandmother—her aunt Vi. They're fascinating. Rather like verbal snapshots of a long-forgotten time."

"You found them?" Tracy felt a rush of pleasure. She'd been dying to read them ever since Dory had asked if she wanted to.

Eric gave a mild snort. "It took us a while, but we did. Frankly, I'm surprised they saved the letters. I mean, they tried to keep everything else so hush-hush. Go figure." He shrugged.

"You should see the sort of things my grandmother kept in her attic," Tracy said with a roll of her eyes.

SECRETS FROM GRANDMA'S ATTIC

Leading the way to his office, Eric said, "I've learned a lot about tuberculosis and the whole sanatorium movement. They treat people with the disease now on an outpatient basis. I went online and found some interesting information about how treatment changed over the years and about the stigma attached to the disease. Some people feared TB victims as though they were lepers."

"Yes, that's an interesting sidebar, isn't?" Tracy replied. "I mean, if there hadn't been the fearful stigma associated with TB, your grandmother—Aunt Vi, as Trula called her—wouldn't have been afraid to invite Trula to visit. She was so embarrassed by her niece's illness and afraid of catching it that one thing led to another, and we ended up with an unnamed woman in the cemetery."

Eric placed the shoebox on his desk and swiped a hand through his hair. "I don't think Trula was well enough to leave the sanatorium, but she did so anyway. She must have caught a cold or something. Her lungs were already compromised, so she came down with pneumonia. Poor girl. She collapsed into a feverish fog and never came to." He met Tracy's sympathetic gaze and sighed heavily.

"Can Annette read the letters too?" Tracy asked. "She and I have been talking about the incident. I think she'd appreciate the opportunity to read what Trula wrote back then—sort of closure for us all."

Eric readily agreed.

When Annette joined them in Eric's office, she ventured to say, "I'm glad to see you in a better mood, Eric. I guess the disappointment of the rejection letter has worn off some."

Pausing in the midst of sipping his coffee, Eric raised an eyebrow. "How'd you know about that?"

Annette shrugged. "I confess, I saw the letter the other day when I came in to put some mail on your desk. It lay there open for anyone to see, so I knew you'd written a book of some sort and that a big New York publisher rejected it. At least it was personalized—not one of those form letters about 'not meeting our present needs' or whatever."

"So you really have written a book?" Tracy pressed.

"I have," Eric admitted. "And yes, I was disappointed about the rejection, but the fact is, I've been more worried about my mother's health and my grandmother's as well." Looking at Tracy, he added, "They are both going downhill, and it hurts to see that happen. Besides, Christmas is a lonely time for me since my divorce. I'm grumpy in December. I guess I've been grumpier than usual." He gave an embarrassed shrug.

"You have been kind of a Scrooge," Annette acknowledged. "But I suppose you've had reason enough. So, this book you've written, is it a novel?"

Eric shook his head. "No. It's a compilation of little-known incidents in Missouri history."

"Were you also researching the Woman in White mystery?" Tracy asked. "I thought you were angry with me because I was looking into the incident too. I thought maybe that's why seeing my grandmother's scrapbook upset you so much."

"No, the topic intrigued me because my sister and I began to piece together our grandmother's connection to the incident," Eric explained. "I don't want to write about it. I would feel as though I was airing my family's dirty laundry for the whole community to see." A flush colored his lean cheeks. "And by the way, thank you,

SECRETS FROM GRANDMA'S ATTIC

Tracy, for letting Granny have the cameo and Trula's suitcase. In her better moments, Granny is delighted to talk about them now. Elaine too. After all, she played a key role in the mystery."

"She did," Tracy acknowledged. She gave Annette a quick summary of what had taken place a few days earlier at the nursing home. To Eric she said, "I told Melody Bailey about returning the suitcase to your grandmother. She and Lincoln are delighted that after all these years, the suitcase and its contents have been returned to the family of the Woman in White—a woman we now know was Trula Drybeck."

"Thank you for giving us your grandmother's scrapbook too," Eric said. "Are you sure your aunt and sister don't want to keep it?"

"I'm sure," Tracy said. "Aunt Ruth is delighted by the outcome and insists her mother—my grandma Pearl—would be tickled pink about how this has all turned out. That's really all my grandmother wanted— to discover the dead woman's identity and notify her family."

"Then the cameo is a family heirloom after all?" Annette asked.

Eric nodded. "Yes. My great-great-grandmother gave it to Grandma Violet's older sister, who in turn gave it to Trula, who wore it when she got married. And now it belongs to my grandmother, Trula's younger cousin. Granny promised to give it to my sister Ann."

"That's a lovely tradition. I'm so glad the brooch has found its way home again," Tracy said happily.

"Thanks to you." Eric smiled. "By the way, we're thinking of giving the suitcase and the scrapbook to Tawny at the historical society. She might be interested in having them, since the incident took place in Canton. Anyway, we'll see."

"What about the letters?" Tracy indicated the shoebox on the corner of his desk.

"We haven't decided what to do with those yet." Eric lifted the lid. "Here, read one."

He passed the open box to Tracy first before offering it to Annette.

Tracy took one of the letters. The paper was fragile and wrinkled with age. The ink had faded. "Look at this handwriting. They had such good penmanship back then."

For nearly half an hour the three sat in companionable silence, drinking coffee and reading Trula Drybeck's letters to her aunt Violet. Tracy felt a tug of sympathy for the young widow who pleaded so longingly to join her family in Canton. The letters were newsy and authentic and sad. She wondered what had happened to the return letters that Violet had written back to her.

"Aunt Violet comes across as rather hard-hearted, don't you think?" Annette observed after reading more than half the letters. "She apparently didn't write often and never once offered an invitation to poor Trula to come visit. She wouldn't even visit her at the sanatorium. The girl mentions the train and bus, practically begging to be invited for Christmas." Then, apparently remembering that Violet was Eric's great-grandmother, Annette hastily added, "Sorry, Eric, no offense meant."

He accepted this with a nod. "None taken. I think I would have felt the same if I hadn't heard my mother's account of Grandma Violet's guilt and shame. And it wasn't uncommon for patients never to have a single visitor because people were so embarrassed or fearful of coming in contact with them while they were sick."

"There was a war going on too," Tracy reminded them. "People were already so fearful. The disease was just one more thing to worry about. I do feel sorry for Trula, but I feel sorry for Violet and Dory too."

Eric cleared his throat. "Granny told me that my great-grandmother was a woman without joy. Granny said she always seemed fretful and worried about something. Of course, she became a widow before she was forty-five years old and had to raise my grandmother on her own. That's never easy. She never remarried either. She worked hard, and now I know that she felt guilty all the rest of her days because she never came forward to identify Trula. She was always afraid that she'd broken a law and might go to jail."

Tracy placed a letter back in the box. "Sadly, Vi passed that guilt and fear on to Dory." She sent up a silent prayer of thanks that Grandma Pearl had been a different sort of woman.

"What a dismal legacy." Annette shook her head. "The poor woman let joy get sucked out of her life."

Eric sighed. "Such a heavy burden."

"But at least Dory had Elaine to confide in," Tracy said. "That had to be a comfort to some extent."

"Elaine has proven to be a true friend to Granny," Eric agreed. "We're grateful. In fact, Ann has invited Elaine and her granddaughter Poppy to join us for Christmas dinner this year. We're bringing Granny home for the day to join in the celebration too."

"That's wonderful," Tracy exclaimed.

"I love happy endings," Annette declared. Turning to Tracy, she added, "Your grandma Pearl would be delighted with how this has all turned out."

Tracy couldn't have agreed more.

Chapter Twenty-Six

Christmas Day dawned gray and cold. The weatherman had predicted snow, but so far there'd only been a dusting, reminding Tracy of the powdered sugar she'd sprinkled over the pan of gingerbread she baked before everyone showed up for the festivities. It was a noisy but joyful morning. The women all took turns cuddling baby Elizabeth while Uncle Martin donned a Santa hat to hand out the presents. The little kids squealed with pleasure, and Amy's youngsters didn't seem to mind receiving pajamas and new underwear and socks from Uncle Jeff and Aunt Tracy. Jana was her usual bubbly self. Tracy felt relieved to see that she and Natalie once again appeared to be the best of chums. But the discovery of the pinball machine, wrapped with a giant red ribbon and hidden in the den, was the highlight of the day. The four older kids—and teenage Kai—had to be ordered more than once by Miles and Terry to come to the table to eat.

Later that afternoon when most everyone had gone home, Tracy drove to the cemetery. There was one last present she wanted to bestow. "Isn't it amazing?" she said, standing beside Trula Drybeck's grave, staring down at the headstone. Amy, Robin, and Aunt Ruth stood next to her. All were bundled up in coats, gloves, and scarves. Shivering, Tracy added, "We finally have a name for the mysterious woman buried here."

"Thanks to your persistence," Aunt Ruth said. In her hands, she held a large bouquet of white roses tied up with red velvet ribbon.

"And thanks to Grandma Pearl's caring heart," Robin added. She stood next to her mother, gently clutching the older woman by the elbow. "If Grandma hadn't kept the scrapbook, if she hadn't served on the committee to make sure this young woman had a suitable burial, Tracy might never have pursued the mystery."

"Your grandmother would be so pleased," Aunt Ruth added with a watery sniff. "And proud of you too, Tracy."

Despite the cold, Tracy felt her cheeks grow warm with pleasure from her aunt's praise.

Aunt Ruth leaned over to place the bouquet on the grave, propping the flowers up against the headstone.

There was a moment of silence before Tracy commented, "When I ordered the bouquet from Fancy Floral, the salesclerk mentioned that someone else had ordered the exact same thing."

Robin raised an eyebrow. "Really? I wonder who?"

"Maybe Melody Bailey," Amy suggested. "She took a keen interest in all of this, didn't she?"

"Or maybe Poppy and her grandmother," Robin suggested. "Poppy hasn't stopped talking about the scrapbook or the cameo since Elaine filled her in on the whole story."

Tracy shrugged as she clutched her hands behind her back. She'd planned to come here alone to the cemetery to place the flowers on the grave as an act of closure. But when Amy, Robin, and Aunt Ruth had learned what she planned to do, they'd offered to come along. Amy explained that it would also serve as a tribute to Grandma Pearl.

The Cameo Clue

Sighing with contentment, Tracy felt a glow of peace. The nameless young woman was nameless no more. Last night's Christmas pageant had gone off without a hitch, and everyone was looking forward to the family Christmas celebration the next day. Tracy could hardly wait to spend time with all of her grandchildren without thoughts of the Woman in White hovering at the back of her mind.

"Poppy thinks this whole incident is as exciting as a made-for-TV movie," Robin said.

They all laughed. "We did have our moments of drama," Tracy said.

Just then Tracy heard a car inching its way slowly down the narrow avenue leading to the grave site. They all turned to look, wondering who had come to the lonely cemetery on this bitterly cold afternoon. The car stopped behind Tracy's vehicle. The headlights blinked off. A man opened the door and emerged from the driver's seat. He carried a floral arrangement in one hand. White roses tied with a red velvet ribbon.

"Isn't that your boss?" Amy murmured.

Tracy nodded. It was indeed Eric Watson. She should have guessed that it was Eric who placed the order for the other bouquet of white roses. As he approached them slowly, almost hesitantly, Tracy raised a gloved hand to greet him.

"Great minds think alike," he quipped as he joined them by the graveside. He pointed to the bouquet that Aunt Ruth had already placed on the grave.

After Tracy made quick introductions all around, she said, "We wanted to pay our respects to Trula on Grandma Pearl's behalf. She would be one hundred and two today, if she was still living. I think

SECRETS FROM GRANDMA'S ATTIC

Grandma would be over the moon that the Woman in White now has a name."

"And a family," Aunt Ruth added with a shy smile.

Eric smiled. Even in the gathering gloom, Tracy could see the flush on his lean cheeks.

"Speaking of names," he said, "my grandmother wants me to see that Trula's is engraved on the stone. That's one reason I came out here today—to see if there's a space where the name can be added. The other reason was to bring these, of course."

"What a lovely idea," Tracy said. She felt pleased for Eric that his grandmother still had her lucid moments. She hoped that Dory realized she no longer had to be afraid. The poor woman had lived with fear and anxiety far too long.

Aunt Ruth pointed at the headstone. "Seems to me there's plenty of room for Trula's name."

"It wouldn't surprise me one bit to learn that Grandma Pearl specifically requested that a space be left so that a name could be added at some later time," Amy put in.

Robin nodded, linking her arm through her mother's. "That's just the sort of thing Grandma Pearl would think of."

Eric squatted down to place his bouquet next to their own. As he rose, he added, "I wish I'd known your grandmother. She must have been a very special lady."

"She sure was," Amy declared.

Aunt Ruth sniffed loudly.

Tracy could feel a lump in her throat. Christmas was always an emotional time. This year seemed even more so as she'd welcomed a new grandbaby into her life and become embroiled in the poignant

Trula Drybeck incident. She blinked rapidly, swiping at the wetness on her cheeks.

Eric said quietly, "I want to thank you, Tracy—all of you—for helping to make this Christmas a very special one for my family. My sister and I are aware that it may be our last holiday celebration with Granny. Her health is failing. It becomes more evident every day. We intend to make the most of our time with her while we can."

"I'm so glad," Tracy said, her voice thick with emotion. Again, she became mindful of something wet on her cheek. She touched it with a gloved hand and then looked up. Snowflakes fluttered gently down from the gloomy sky.

"It's snowing!" Amy declared with delight. "I know some kids who are going to be absolutely thrilled."

"I need to go," Eric announced. "My sister is expecting me for supper. Merry Christmas, ladies. And thanks again." He gave them a mock salute.

"Merry Christmas," they chorused.

"It's getting colder," Robin observed. "Let's get you home, Mom, before you turn into an icicle."

Aunt Ruth laughed and allowed Robin and Amy to lead her back to Tracy's vehicle.

Tracy paused a moment beside the grave, looking down one last time at the floral tributes. She was delighted that Eric's family would see to the adding of Trula's name to the headstone. How she loved happy endings!

"Merry Christmas, Trula," she murmured with a contented sigh. "And happy birthday, Grandma Pearl."

Dear Friends,

I hope you have enjoyed Tracy and Amy's latest adventure. The story is a rather personal one for me. My aunt Millie was diagnosed with tuberculosis many years ago. She was admitted to a sanatorium for the "fresh air and wholesome food" cure. She had to leave behind a husband and three small children.

You can imagine how stressful that was for all concerned. My grandmother moved in to help take care of the youngsters for several months until their mother could return home. Some patients, unable or unwilling to abide by the strict rules and regulations, walked out of the facilities. Others, like Trula in this story, became so homesick, they left, not realizing—or not caring—that they were contagious.

Fortunately, those contracting tuberculosis today can be treated on an outpatient basis.

If you've ever had a friend or relative who was admitted to a sanatorium after being diagnosed with TB, you may be interested to know that many of these medical institutions—although they are now closed—have websites with photographs and patient memoirs. I perused several while writing this novel and became fascinated by the personal stories posted there.

Good health is a blessing. I think you'll agree. My prayer is that you and yours will always enjoy good health and a happy heart. As the Bible says in Proverbs 17:22, "A cheerful heart is good medicine." You can bet that Grandma Pearl quoted that verse often to her loved ones!

Yours truly,
Shirley Raye

About The Author

Shirley Raye Redmond has received numerous awards for both her women's fiction and her children's books. Her devotions have appeared in multiple volumes of Guideposts' *All God's Creatures* and *Daily Guideposts,* and she has enjoyed writing several mysteries for Guideposts' Savannah Secrets series. Shirley Raye has been married for forty-eight years to her college sweetheart. They live in the scenic mountains of northern New Mexico. When not writing, she enjoys birdwatching, even traveling to Iceland to photograph Atlantic puffins and sailing to the Bahamas to enjoy getting up close and personal with flamingos.

COLLECTIBLES *from* GRANDMA'S ATTIC

Cameos

While writing *The Cameo Clue*, I kept a cameo pin beside my computer. It was a gift from my grandmother years ago, and she had received it from her mother. As you know, a cameo is a small stone with a silhouette of a carved face overlaid on it. These types of silhouettes were first introduced in eastern Asia more than a thousand years ago when they were used as wax stamps to securely seal letters. Sometimes cameos served as medals to show the high rank of the people who wore them. Cameos were also attached to drinking cups.

The Greeks carved such beautiful cameos that people wore them as ornaments on brooches, earrings, pins, bracelets, and even rings. Fine cameos are carved from semiprecious stones such as sardonyx and agate. It takes a skilled jeweler to carve such a piece. Less expensive ones are made from glass or seashells.

Queen Victoria and Pope Paul II were avid collectors of cameos. Today, some of the most beautiful are carved in Rome, Italy. So before you toss out Grandma Gertie's old jewelry, make sure you're not throwing away a vintage cameo. While browsing eBay recently, I discovered several selling for nearly $500!

SOMETHING DELICIOUS *From* GRANDMA
PEARL'S RECIPE BOX

TRACY'S PEPPERMINT PIE

Ingredients:

3 pints (1½ quarts) peppermint ice cream

1 ready-made chocolate-cookie piecrust

1 (12 ounce) jar hot fudge sauce

Directions:

In a chilled bowl, stir ice cream until softened.

Spoon ice cream into piecrust. Spread evenly.

Place in freezer for 4 hours.

To serve, let pie stand at room temperature for five minutes.

Warm hot fudge topping in microwave.

Pour topping over pie and sprinkle with crushed peppermint
candies, if desired.

Makes 8 servings.

*Read on for a sneak peek of another exciting book
in the Secrets from Grandma's Attic series!*

Veiled Intentions
By Gabrielle Meyer

A gentle snow fell from the dark clouds outside Amy Allen's house. The temperature had fallen throughout the day, but Amy hardly noticed as she sat at the cozy dinner table with her combined family. Her fiancé, Miles Anderson, met her gaze from across the table, and they shared a quiet smile. Their children competed to tell them about the snowball fight that had left them all rosy-faced and happy.

"The girls won," seven-year-old Jana said, making a face at the boys. Jana was Amy's adopted daughter, and she was the same age as Miles's daughter, Natalie. The two girls were best friends and already called themselves sisters, although the wedding was still three weeks away.

"No way," Matt said. He looked to Colton for confirmation. "We threw more snowballs and hit you more than you hit us."

Matt was Jana's brother, and he and Colton were both eleven and in the same class at Canton Elementary School. Though their relationship had gotten off to a rocky start, they were good friends now. Maybe not as excited to become brothers as the girls were to become sisters, but they still looked forward to the new family adventure.

"I don't think it really matters who won," Miles said. "I'm just happy you were outside enjoying yourselves. What else did you do in the snow?"

Natalie began to tell him all about the snow angels she and Jana had made, while the boys talked about building snowmen.

Amy watched and listened, marveling that in three short weeks she, Matt, and Jana would move in with Miles and his kids and they'd start their lives together. Finally. After dating in high school and then breaking up before going to college, Amy and Miles had gone their separate ways for over thirty years. But both had returned to their hometown of Canton, Missouri, about the same time. Amy as a single mom to two adopted children and Miles as a single, divorced dad. Their friendship had quickly rekindled, though their romance had taken a little more time to develop. But Amy wouldn't change a thing. It had all happened exactly how God had orchestrated, and they would soon be married.

"Who's ready for dessert?" Amy asked when she heard the oven timer ding. The noise made Scrappy bark. Miles and Amy had recently purchased the little black, white, and brown ball of fur with floppy ears. He had been enjoying shared company with both families but would soon live full-time with the whole family at Miles's house.

A unanimous chorus rose to accompany Scrappy's barks.

"I'll help," Miles said. He stood and joined Amy in the kitchen.

The kids continued to talk in animated voices about the snow, hoping more would fall over the weekend so that school would be canceled on Monday morning.

"Supper was great," Miles said as he went to the freezer and took out the vanilla ice cream he had brought to Amy's house for their dessert.

Amy opened the oven and pulled out the pan of brownies, shooing Scrappy away. The chocolate aroma filled the kitchen and made her stomach rumble, despite just having eaten supper.

"Thanks." Amy knew Miles loved lasagna, so she had made it just for him.

"I see you've started to pack." Miles motioned to a stack of boxes near the back door.

"Those are things I'm donating to the thrift store, but I have started to pack." She couldn't hide her excitement as she set the brownies on the counter.

Miles approached her and slipped his arms around her, pulling her close.

Amy hugged him back. They would be living in the same house together in three short weeks. Miles's home was a large Victorian, not far from her sister Tracy. It was easily twice as big as Amy's house and filled with so many good memories already. She would miss this house, but she was eager to make a new home.

"I'm literally crossing the days off on my calendar," Miles said with a grin.

Amy smiled and left his arms to take a knife out of the drawer to cut the brownies. "I signed papers with the Realtor yesterday. She said that things are a little slow right now, but she's hopeful that by

SECRETS FROM GRANDMA'S ATTIC

spring we'll have the house sold. I let her know we're not in any hurry. As long as we get the necessities moved into your house by the wedding, we can take our time moving the rest out afterward. I won't mind if it takes a little bit of time to sell my house."

Amy cut into the brownies though they were still piping hot. She lifted the gooey dessert into serving bowls, and Miles dropped a scoop of ice cream into each. They carried them into the dining room and were met with cheers.

Everyone made quick work of the dessert, and then the kids cleared their plates. They took Scrappy into the living room, where they attempted to teach him how to sit, roll over, and fetch, leaving Miles and Amy at the table to talk.

They were discussing wedding plans when Amy's phone rang.

Amy stood and returned to the kitchen where her cell phone was charging on the counter. When she picked it up, she saw her Realtor's number.

"Hello?" she said.

"Hi, Amy, this is Carol Molenkamp."

"Hi, Carol. How are you?"

"I'm great—perfect, actually. I have some wonderful news for you."

"Oh?"

"You got an offer on your house today!"

Amy frowned, confused. "What do you mean? You haven't even shown it yet."

"The buyer contacted me this morning, looking for a house that fit the description of yours perfectly. She lives in Florida and doesn't have the opportunity to come and see it in person, so I sent her the pictures I took yesterday. She loved it and made a cash offer."

The Cameo Clue

It took Amy a moment to process everything Carol had just said. She left the kitchen and joined Miles in the dining room. He looked at her curiously.

"There's been an offer on the house," Amy said to him.

He grinned and gave her a thumbs-up.

"The buyer is offering above asking price too," Carol continued.

"What?" Amy could hardly believe it.

"But there's a catch." Carol's voice grew serious.

"Okay." Amy took the seat across from Miles and said, "Carol, can I put you on speaker so Miles can listen in?"

"Of course."

Amy lowered her phone and placed it on speaker. "Go ahead, Carol."

"Sure. I was just telling Amy that she's had a cash offer on her house from a buyer in Florida. The buyer has offered above asking price, but there's a caveat." She paused and took a deep breath. "She'll need you to close on the house in two weeks."

Amy's jaw dropped. "Two weeks? That's impossible. We're getting married in three weeks, and I'm in the middle of planning the wedding. I couldn't possibly move out of my house in two weeks. Couldn't we make it at least a month?"

"The buyer needs the house in two weeks. She's moving from Florida and needs somewhere to live when she gets here. It's a non-negotiable closing date."

Amy looked at Miles.

He simply shrugged.

"Carol, can Miles and I discuss this and call you back?"

"Of course. I'll email you the details, and you can take some time to talk things through. I'll need an answer by tomorrow morning though, because if you aren't willing to accept the offer, then the buyer will need to keep looking. She has a job starting here in two weeks."

"I understand. Thanks. I'll let you know first thing in the morning."

"Okay. Bye, you two. I look forward to hearing from you."

"Bye," Amy and Miles both said before Amy ended the call.

Amy studied Miles as he smiled at her.

"Wow," he said, "that was unexpected."

Amy took a deep breath. "I don't even know what to say. I didn't think this would happen so quickly."

"The offer is great," Miles said. "And the extra money would be nice."

"I have been wanting to start a college fund for Matt and Jana." Amy paused. "For all the kids."

Miles reached across the table and took her hand. "It takes some getting used to, doesn't it? The idea of sharing everything. Finances, kids, plans—"

"Dreams," she finished with a smile, and then grew serious again. "Do you think we could move out of here in two weeks? There's so much to do with the wedding and moving into your house—I'm not sure it's possible."

"I'm free every evening," he said. "And we can ask your family for help. I know Tracy and Robin will be here every opportunity they can get."

Amy's sister, Tracy, and their cousin, Robin, were her two best friends. If she asked them, she knew they'd help.

"It sounds like you think this is a good idea," she said.

He let go of her hand and nodded. "I know it'll be tough, but I think we can do it. I don't want to miss an opportunity for you to sell the house for top dollar. I think it'll be worth the extra work in the end."

Amy nibbled her bottom lip. If she was doing it by herself, she'd have to say no. But with Miles's help, and the possibility of her sister and cousin's help too, she felt more confident.

"Okay. I'll let Carol know in the morning that we'll accept the offer. And I'll see if the kids and I can stay with Tracy and Jeff for the week between the sale and the wedding. She has lots of space, and I know she won't mind."

Miles grinned and stood.

He reached out to Amy, and she stood. "Congratulations," he said as he pulled her close. "We're about to be a one-home family."

Amy laid her cheek against Miles's chest, excited and a little apprehensive. It was all happening so quickly. She just hoped she didn't regret saying yes to the offer.

Amy felt distracted the next morning as she entered the church with Matt and Jana for Sunday school. The kids ran off to their classrooms and Amy hung her jacket on the coatrack.

"Hey," Tracy said as she came up behind Amy. "What's this about you selling your house?"

Amy turned to her older sister just as their cousin, Robin, walked up to join them.

"You sold your house?" Robin asked with big eyes.

"How did you hear?" Amy asked Tracy.

"Jana just told me as she ran by me on her way to class."

Amy smiled and shook her head. "She's like the town crier."

"Is it true?" Robin asked.

"It's true. I called Carol Molenkamp this morning before we came to church." Amy quickly filled them in on the particulars.

"How are you feeling?" Tracy asked.

"A little worried and apprehensive," Amy admitted. "But also excited and ready to be done and move on to the next phase of my life."

Miles entered the church with Colton and Natalie. The kids ran off to their classrooms while Miles joined Amy, Tracy, and Robin.

"Amy just told us the good news," Tracy said to Miles after everyone greeted each other. "I say we should all head over to Amy's right after Sunday lunch to get started on packing."

"You guys don't need to come over on your day off," Amy protested.

"I'll pretty much be at your house every waking minute these next two weeks," Tracy warned. "And Jeff will help when he can. We have a lot of work to do."

Amy didn't realize just how much she was hoping her sister would help. Relief flooded her, and she gave Tracy a big hug. "Thank you."

"Of course."

The morning went by quickly, and soon Amy, Miles, and the kids pulled up to Tracy's house for their weekly Sunday meal.

Tracy and her husband, Jeff, had inherited Grandma Pearl's beautiful Victorian home when Grandma passed away two years ago. In the recently fallen snow, it was especially beautiful. A large turret, bay windows, and a wraparound porch were some of the

The Cameo Clue

features that made it remarkable, but it was the years of family memories within that made it special. Tracy and Jeff were the third generation to own the home, and it was full of priceless treasures and mysteries from decades of family life.

The kids greeted each other after they pulled up in two different vehicles as if they hadn't just spent the morning together at church. They ran into the house even before Amy and Miles had met on the sidewalk out front.

Miles reached for Amy's hand, and they walked to the house together.

Tracy greeted them at the door with a big smile. "Come on in. Lunch will be ready soon."

Robin was already there with her husband, Terry, and their fifteen-year-old son, Kai. Miles and Amy took off their outer gear, and Matt, Colton, and Kai left to find a board game to play.

"It smells delicious in here," Amy said.

"Jeff made his famous meat loaf," Tracy said. "I'm making mashed potatoes and gravy."

"I brought a salad," Robin added.

"And I have dessert," Amy said. She held up the pan of chocolate cake she had made the previous night and frosted that morning.

"Great." Tracy stood back and waited until everyone had their coats hung up. "Miles and Terry, I'm wondering if you'd be willing to help Jeff out in the kitchen while I take Amy and Robin on a little treasure hunt in the attic."

"Oh?" Amy handed Miles the chocolate cake. "What kind of treasure hunt?"

Tracy shrugged. "It's a secret."

Amy frowned, curious about what her sister was up to.

Miles winked at her as he left the foyer and moved toward the kitchen with Terry at his side.

Robin and Amy followed Tracy up the stairs to the second floor.

"What is this about?" Robin asked Tracy. "I had a feeling you didn't want to say anything in front of the guys."

Tracy smiled as she walked toward the guest room. The stairs to the attic were inside the bedroom closet.

"There are only three weeks until Amy's wedding," Tracy said with her hand on the doorknob. "And now that we're going to be busy packing up her house, I thought we better find the family veil to get it aired out for the wedding."

Amy paused before she entered the room, her heart warming. "I almost forgot! How could I forget?"

Tracy and Robin smiled at Amy—their excitement for her wedding almost as keen as hers.

The family wedding veil had first been worn by Great-grandma Vivian at her wedding. It was a gorgeous veil with a delicate, pearl-lined headpiece and long, cathedral-length netting. After Great-grandma Vivian wore it, Grandma Pearl had worn it, and her daughter, Ruth—Robin's mother—had been the third bride. Both Robin and Tracy had worn it, and the last to wear it was Tracy's daughter, Sara.

"You'll be the seventh bride to wear the veil," Tracy said, smiling at Amy. "Six very happy marriages have preceded you—and I know the seventh will be just as joyful and blessed."

Tears sprang to Amy's eyes.

The Cameo Clue

The bedroom light was turned on, and the closet door was already open. The sound of Jana and Natalie's giggles could be heard coming from the attic.

"It sounds like the girls have beat us to it," Tracy said.

"Remember when we used to play up there?" Amy asked.

"Some of my happiest memories took place up there," Robin said. "Playing dress-up in Grandma Pearl's old bridesmaid dresses."

The three of them walked up the steep steps to the attic. A bare lightbulb hung overhead, and piles of furniture, covered with dust-covers, were scattered throughout the room. There were boxes, rubber storage bins, old trunks filled with treasures, and several generations of family heirlooms.

"What are you two doing up here?" Amy asked when she got to the top of the stairs.

"We're playing with Grandma Pearl's dollhouse," Natalie said with a grin.

Robin and Tracy smiled at Amy, and she could almost tell what they were thinking. They loved that Natalie already thought of Grandma Pearl as her own, even though Miles and Amy weren't married yet.

"What are you doing up here?" Jana asked as she moved one of the dolls from the parlor to the dining room.

"We're up here looking for a very special wedding veil," Tracy said. She moved to a bookcase where several family photo albums were stored. "I'll show you some pictures of it."

The girls went to Tracy's side and waited for her to find the right album. When she did, she took a seat on one of the cloth-covered chairs and opened it for them.

SECRETS FROM GRANDMA'S ATTIC

"This is your great-great-grandmother Vivian," Tracy said, pointing to the picture of Vivian in her wedding dress and veil.

"Oh, she's pretty," Natalie said. "But she looks kind of weird."

"This picture was taken over a hundred years ago. They dressed differently than us, didn't they?" Tracy asked.

The girls nodded.

"This is the veil she wore on her wedding day," Tracy said. "And then…" She flipped a few pages and showed them Grandma Pearl. "Your great-grandma Pearl wore it when she got married in 1945. And then"—she turned another page—"Aunt Ruth wore it, and I wore it, and Robin wore it, and Sara wore it."

The girls' eyes were wide as they studied the pictures.

Natalie looked up at Tracy. "Can I wear it some day?"

"And me?" Jana asked.

Tracy grinned at the girls and nodded. "Of course!"

Amy's heart warmed at the scene.

"Where is it?" Natalie asked.

"It's in the trunk over there." Tracy rose and led the girls to the wedding trunk in the corner of the attic. "We're taking it out so Amy can wear it on her wedding day."

The little girls looked up at Amy with wide eyes.

Inside the wedding trunk they'd stored Great-grandma Vivian's and Grandma Pearl's wedding gowns along with the veil and a few other odds and ends. Amy hadn't seen the veil since Sara's wedding, six years ago, but she remembered it well.

"Sara's wedding was the last one that Grandma Pearl attended," Amy suddenly realized. "I wish she could be here for mine."

"At least you have her veil," Jana said.

Amy chuckled at the simple response. "You're right. Grandma Pearl is here with us through our memories."

Tracy moved some framed pictures off the top of the trunk and opened the lid. It squeaked on its hinges and revealed several boxes within.

Slowly, she removed each box and set them aside, but then she paused.

"I don't see the veil box."

"What?" Amy frowned, getting closer. "What do you mean?"

"It's not in here."

"Maybe it got put in one of the other boxes inside the trunk," Robin suggested.

Tracy, Amy, and Robin opened each box, revealing gowns, gloves, shoes, and other items, but there was no veil.

"How is this possible?" Tracy asked. "I know I returned the veil to this trunk after Sara wore it. I remember specifically. I had it professionally cleaned and stored in an archival box, and then I brought it up here and put it in this trunk."

Robin shrugged. "Maybe it got moved."

"Where?" Tracy asked. "And who would have moved it?"

"I don't know," Robin said. "Maybe Grandma Pearl?"

Disappointment weighed heavily on Amy's heart. All her life, she'd been looking forward to the day she might wear the wedding veil. What if they couldn't find it?

"Did someone steal it?" Jana asked, frowning and clearly upset.

"Surely not." Tracy shook her head. "Who would want to steal the family wedding veil? It can't have any monetary value. It's more of a priceless family heirloom."

SECRETS FROM GRANDMA'S ATTIC

"Something happened to it," Amy said. "It couldn't have just disappeared into thin air. Someone must know where it went."

Robin nodded. "We'll find it, Amy. You're right, it has to be somewhere."

Amy couldn't help but wonder what she would wear if they couldn't find the veil in time.

But, more importantly, where had it gone?

A Note from the Editors

We hope you enjoyed Secrets from Grandma's Attic series, published by Guideposts. For over seventy-five years, Guideposts, a nonprofit organization, has been driven by a vision of a world filled with hope. We aspire to be the voice of a trusted friend, a friend who makes you feel more hopeful and connected.

By making a purchase from Guideposts, you join our community in touching millions of lives, inspiring them to believe that all things are possible through faith, hope, and prayer. Your continued support allows us to provide uplifting resources to those in need. Whether through our communities, websites, apps, or publications, we inspire our audiences, bring them together, and comfort, uplift, entertain, and guide them. Visit us at guideposts.org to learn more.

We would love to hear from you. Write us at Guideposts, P.O. Box 5815, Harlan, Iowa 51593 or call us at (800) 932-2145. Did you love *The Cameo Clue*? Leave a review for this product on guideposts.org/shop. Your feedback helps others in our community find relevant products.

Find inspiration, find faith, find Guideposts.

Shop our best sellers and favorites at
guideposts.org/shop

Or scan the QR code to go directly to our Shop

**While you are waiting for the next fascinating story
in Secrets from Grandma's Attic, check out
some other Guideposts mystery series!**

Savannah Secrets

Welcome to Savannah, Georgia, a picture-perfect Southern city known for its manicured parks, moss-covered oaks, and antebellum architecture. Walk down one of the cobblestone streets, and you'll come upon Magnolia Investigations. It is here where two friends have joined forces to unravel some of Savannah's deepest secrets. Tag along as clues are exposed, red herrings discarded, and thrilling surprises revealed. Find inspiration in the special bond between Meredith Bellefontaine and Julia Foley. Cheer the friends on as they listen to their hearts and rely on their faith to solve each new case that comes their way.

The Hidden Gate
A Fallen Petal
Double Trouble
Whispering Bells
Where Time Stood Still
The Weight of Years
Willful Transgressions

Season's Meetings
Southern Fried Secrets
The Greatest of These
Patterns of Deception
The Waving Girl
Beneath a Dragon Moon
Garden Variety Crimes
Meant for Good
A Bone to Pick
Honeybees & Legacies
True Grits
Sapphire Secret
Jingle Bell Heist
Buried Secrets
A Puzzle of Pearls
Facing the Facts
Resurrecting Trouble
Forever and a Day

Mysteries of Martha's Vineyard

Priscilla Latham Grant has inherited a lighthouse! So with not much more than a strong will and a sore heart, the recent widow says goodbye to her lifelong Kansas home and heads to the quaint and historic island of Martha's Vineyard, Massachusetts. There, she comes face-to-face with adventures, which include her trusty canine friend, Jake, three delightful cousins she didn't know she had, and Gerald O'Bannon, a handsome Coast Guard captain—plus head-scratching mysteries that crop up with surprising regularity.

A Light in the Darkness
Like a Fish Out of Water
Adrift
Maiden of the Mist
Making Waves
Don't Rock the Boat
A Port in the Storm
Thicker Than Water
Swept Away
Bridge Over Troubled Waters
Smoke on the Water
Shifting Sands

SECRETS FROM GRANDMA'S ATTIC

Shark Bait
Seascape in Shadows
Storm Tide
Water Flows Uphill
Catch of the Day
Beyond the Sea
Wider Than an Ocean
Sheeps Passing in the Night
Sail Away Home
Waves of Doubt
Lifeline
Flotsam & Jetsam
Just Over the Horizon

Miracles & Mysteries of Mercy Hospital

Four talented women from very different walks of life witness the miracles happening around them at Mercy Hospital and soon become fast friends. Join Joy Atkins, Evelyn Perry, Anne Mabry, and Shirley Bashore as, together, they solve the puzzling mysteries that arise at this Charleston, South Carolina, historic hospital—rumored to be under the protection of a guardian angel. Come along as our quartet of faithful friends solve mysteries, stumble upon a few of the hospital's hidden and forgotten passageways, and discover historical treasures along the way! This fast-paced series is filled with inspiration, adventure, mystery, delightful humor, and loads of Southern charm!

Where Mercy Begins
Prescription for Mystery
Angels Watching Over Me
A Change of Art
Conscious Decisions
Surrounded by Mercy
Broken Bonds
Mercy's Healing
To Heal a Heart

SECRETS FROM GRANDMA'S ATTIC

A Cross to Bear
Merciful Secrecy
Sunken Hopes
Hair Today, Gone Tomorrow
Pain Relief
Redeemed by Mercy
A Genius Solution
A Hard Pill to Swallow
Ill at Ease
'Twas the Clue Before Christmas

Find more inspiring stories in these best-loved Guideposts fiction series!

Mysteries of Lancaster County

Follow the Classen sisters as they unravel clues and uncover hidden secrets in Mysteries of Lancaster County. As you get to know these women and their friends, you'll see how God brings each of them together for a fresh start in life.

Secrets of Wayfarers Inn

Retired schoolteachers find themselves owners of an old warehouse-turned-inn that is filled with hidden passages, buried secrets, and stunning surprises that will set them on a course to puzzling mysteries from the Underground Railroad.

Tearoom Mysteries Series

Mix one stately Victorian home, a charming lakeside town in Maine, and two adventurous cousins with a passion for tea and hospitality. Add a large scoop of intriguing mystery, and sprinkle generously with faith, family, and friends, and you have the recipe for *Tearoom Mysteries*.

Ordinary Women of the Bible

Richly imagined stories—based on facts from the Bible—have all the plot twists and suspense of a great mystery, while bringing you fascinating insights on what it was like to be a woman living in the ancient world.

To learn more about these books, visit Guideposts.org/Shop